UNTIL IT HURTS

Until It Hurts

America's Obsession with Youth Sports
and How It Harms Our Kids

Mark Hyman

Beacon Press
Boston

Beacon Press
25 Beacon Street
Boston, Massachusetts 02108-2892
www.beacon.org

Beacon Press books
are published under the auspices of
the Unitarian Universalist Association of Congregations.

17 16 15 14   8 7 6 5

This book is printed on acid-free paper that meets the uncoated paper
ANSI/NISO specifications for permanence as revised in 1992.

Text design by Tag Savage at Wilsted & Taylor Publishing Services

Library of Congress Cataloging-in-Publication Data
Hyman, Mark.
  Until it hurts : America's obsession with youth sports and how it harms
  our kids / Mark Hyman.
    p. cm.
  ISBN-13: 978-0-8070-2119-4 (paperback : alk. paper)
    1. Sports for children—United States.   2. Sports for children—Social
aspects—United States.   3. Sports for children—United States—
Psychological aspects.   I. Title.
  GV709.2.H96 2009
  796.083—dc22   2008037133

For Peggy

CONTENTS

INTRODUCTION

Recently, I came across an old photo of my son Ben, then eighteen months old, taken in our front yard. On what appears to be the coldest day of the year in Baltimore, he's bundled in a snowsuit and knit cap, his red face barely visible behind layers of fleece and goose down. All around him is a blanket of fresh snow.

It's a classic wintry scene that would make for an excellent holiday greeting card, except for one unsettling feature: Ben is posed beside a batting tee. Grasped in his red mittens is a plastic bat. On an ideal day for ice fishing, my toddler was in the yard taking batting practice.

Whose idea was it to hone the swing of a toddler in the dead of winter? Mine. What was I thinking? I wish I had an answer. Looking back, nineteen years farther along, I can't imagine what was going through my mind. That this was a good idea? That this was appropriate? That midwinter practice would somehow give my son an edge down the road? Blissfully, I have no memory of what delusion I was entertaining that frigid day.

I begin with that rather humbling anecdote as a sort of confession. Not only am I writing about the problems plaguing youth sports in America, for a long time I have done my part to perpetuate them.

Here are my credentials: I am the father of two sons, each of whom played organized sports. For fifteen years I attended their practices, games, postseason tournaments, and team parties with the punctuality of a school principal.

I cared deeply about their successes and setbacks in athletics. Too deeply. I am not one of those adults who becomes notorious for spectacularly inappropriate acts at youth sports games—like the overheated father who ensured his son's defeat in a high school wrestling match by leaping onto the mat and attempting to pin his boy's startled opponent—but watching one of my sons' games can be a trial for me. (Not watching is the only thing that's worse.) Years ago, I decided that it was best if I stood off on my own, separate from other parents. Once the game begins, I'm not good company.

Early in my children's sports lives, I transitioned from anonymous dad in the bleachers to volunteer dad. At various times, I served as coach of the Barons, Mustangs, Jets, and Elite Giants. I was a league board member, seemingly in charge of dissenting each year on the need to give a special award for the best player in the league. Then for two years, I was the commissioner of a local youth league with a staggering 850 players. It was more a full-time job than my full-time job. I have been a contributor to the youth sports economy, having spent lavishly on various summer camps, clinics, showcase events, and private tutors.

Finally, I have written numerous articles about youth sports as a reporter and, for the past eleven years, a contributing editor at *BusinessWeek*. Over the years, I've reported on the big business of Little League Baseball, the cottage industry of one-on-one sports lessons, and other such topics. Then in 2004, I stumbled on a story in equal parts fascinating and disturbing. My good friend Charles Silberstein, the retired team physician for the Baltimore Orioles, had recently returned from a medical conference. He had attended a presentation given by a colleague, Dr. James Andrews, a renowned orthopedic surgeon whose sports medicine clinic in Birmingham, Alabama, is a haven for professional athletes. At the conference, Andrews had shared unpublished data about a growing number of high school ballplayers who had been showing up in his office with a devastating elbow injury—a rupture of the ulnar collateral ligament. The players, many just fifteen and sixteen years old, had come to see him in hopes of having Tommy John surgery, a ghoulish operation in which a tendon from the patient's wrist or leg is used to take the place of a useless elbow ligament.

I wrote an article with the headline "Tommy John Comes to High School," citing Dr. Andrews's statistics and raising questions about the adults who failed to keep the injured pitchers safe. About the parents, I wondered, had dreams of college scholarships and even big pro contracts totally overtaken their judgment? Of the coaches I asked, what did it say about their priorities that a bunch of fifteen-year-olds needed new elbows?

Not even two years later, I was seeing the issue through a far different lens. By then, with my son in the doctor's waiting room, I had become the overzealous parent and the accuser had become the accused. I was eager to share that turn of events as well. First, I needed permission from my son Ben. In a leap of faith and without conditions, he gave me the go-ahead. Thank you, Ben.

This book, then, seeks to tell the story of adults and their role in shaping youth sports in America today. It's a story of moms and daughters as much as dads and sons, of field hockey and girls lacrosse as much as baseball or football. It's not a flattering account, and it doesn't have an entirely happy ending. My hope is that it sparks debate about the proper role for grownups and advocates for a more kid-centric approach to games that, after all, are supposed to be about kids.

■ ■ ■

Across the country, young players are all too frequent victims of a sports culture that seemingly is turning its back on them. Injuries are just one troubling manifestation. With each passing season youth sports seems to stray further and further from its core mission of providing healthy, safe, and character-building recreation for children. Rather, sports for kids has evolved (and devolved) into a playground for those who invited themselves to the games and, like irritating dinner guests, refuse to leave the party—parents, coaches, and other interested adults.

By anyone's reckoning, adults rule youth sports. At the field, gym, rink, or pool, we are the fans, groundskeepers, timekeepers, official scorers, food-stand attendants, travel-team coordinators, raffle chairs, league presidents, and, of course, coaches. At home, our titles are appointment secretaries, chauffeurs, washerwomen (and washermen), short-order cooks, personal shoppers, and human ATMs.

It's not the presence of adults that is distorting youth sports. Rather, the issue is our well-documented impulse to turn sports for children into a de facto professional league. For adults, it seems the fewer distinctions between playing fields for pros and kids, the better. Already we've turned youth sports into highly rated prime-time TV programming worth millions of dollars to networks and their sponsors. Of course, there's the Little League World Series, an annual rite of late summer. Every one of the games appears on ESPN, the national cable channel, and is seen by hundreds of thousands of people. Or how about youth sports as the launching point for reality TV and prime-time drama. NBC scored with critics with *Friday Night Lights,* an adaptation of Buzz Bissinger's tale of high school football in Odessa, Texas. Even MTV got into the act with *Two-a-Days,* a multipart reality show centering on the Hoover, Alabama, scholastic football team and its hard-charging, self-important coach.

Equipping and training youth players also has gone pro. It's just a matter of how much adults are willing to spend. Velocity Sports Performance, based in Alpharetta, Georgia, operates more than seventy gyms around the country. As many as 130,000 kids visit a Velocity gym each year, paying as much as $45 per session to hone their strength, speed, and agility.

Sports psychologists are a must for parents seeking to help their young players eliminate negative thoughts on the starting blocks or pommel horse. A one-hour phone consult with a therapist is just $225. Or consider signing up a child for a private lesson with a former pro athlete. And wait, there's more. When money truly is no object, there are the IMG Academies in Bradenton, Florida, a posh boarding school where young players attend classes in the morning and spend afternoons training in their sports. About seven hundred students, ages ten to eighteen, attend. For some, tuition and sports training exceeds $100,000 a year.

The bigger is better model of youth sports delights adults. We see our kids improve their skills and join highly competitive travel teams, a feat that impresses friends in the neighborhood and validates our superior parenting. The thousands of adults whose living depends on the billion-dollar youth sports economy—selling gear, services, hotel rooms, and such—also are happy. As the wheels of commerce spin, these people also win.

Only kids are losers here. Their voices are rarely heard, and then only to justify the questionable judgments of adults. It's not surprising that children lose their enthusiasm for organized sports, drifting away from such activities or dropping them completely. Training is too intense. Games are too pressurized. Demanding coaches and parents who expect their children to perform as stars and win college scholarships have taken the fun out of the games.

Dr. Lyle Micheli, founder of the first pediatric sports medicine clinic in the United States, at Children's Hospital Boston, says he frequently sees young patients suffering burnout. He just doesn't realize it right away because the patient's initial complaint is of some physical injury—a sore knee or tender shoulder.

When the injury fails to improve as expected after several weeks, it can signal that the patient isn't motivated to return to his or her sport. "This can often be their escape ticket from the whole process," says Micheli.

That the young patients are unable or unwilling to tell their parents that they want to stop playing is revealing. Some have stayed in their sport long after they wanted to quit because they anguished over announcing their decision at home. "Kids are smart enough to know that their parents really like the idea that they're playing soccer, and you just don't quit," Micheli says. "If you walked up to your parents at the dinner table and said, 'I am sick of soccer, I don't want to play anymore,' who knows? They might break down and cry."

1   HOSTILE TAKEOVER

Dalton Carriker swung as hard as a twelve-year-old can swing. The baseball pinged off the metal bat and hung in the air for what seemed like an hour before disappearing over the dark green wall in right field. At a ballpark in Williamsport, Pennsylvania, forty thousand spectators screamed. A global television audience of 70 million sat glued to their sofas. Wearing a grin that exposed his braces, Carriker circled the bases, celebrating the home run that won his team the 2007 Little League World Series presented by Kellogg's Frosted Flakes.

Carl Stotz would have hated it. He wasn't a grinch. Nor was he was opposed to kids playing baseball for fun. Far from it. The founder of Little League Baseball had dedicated his life to that very proposition. As the story goes, Stotz was playing catch in his backyard with his young nephews when one threw a ball wildly. Stotz reached out for the baseball and caught a lilac bush instead. The shrub tore through his sock and skinned his ankle. When the ache subsided, what remained was a big idea: a little league for youth baseball players in which rules, equipment, and life lessons were designed to suit them.

Stotz started the first Little League baseball team in the

spring of 1939. In many ways, he was an unlikely person to launch a revolution in organized youth sports. A bookkeeper for a lumberyard in Williamsport, he looked like a man who spent most of his time indoors—thin and pale. A tuft of wavy brown hair perpetually rose from the top of his head. Though he enjoyed playing baseball as a boy on the local sandlots, he wasn't particularly athletic. His children couldn't even play in the youth baseball league he was creating because both were girls.

Stotz was a dreamer, though, and he needed to be. In his day, the idea of parents and other interested adults banding together to organize a youth sports league was decidedly rare and, in many towns in the United States, unheard of. Children played sports everywhere of course. (During Abraham Lincoln's term as president, a group of boys chose the White House lawn for a game of baseball. Guards shooed them away but Lincoln invited them back.) Adults weren't necessary and, for the most part, were too busy to hang around and watch.

While parents were largely absent from the sports lives of their children, other adults—namely educators, recreation leaders, and youth counselors—were present. In the 1880s, athletics for children thrived in public schools, YMCAs, and under the auspices of other religious and public institutions such as the Boy Scouts and the Boys' Club. Dr. James Naismith, the inventor of basketball, was associated with the YMCA of Springfield, Massachusetts, when he famously nailed up the first peach basket in 1891. (Thus, the National Basketball Hall of Fame is located there.) Naismith's purpose had been to create a game that would be played indoors and could hold the attention of young players over the winter months, enticing them to visit the YMCA year-round.

These organized sports games were about fun and recreation and, for the winners, neighborhood bragging rights. But there were larger purposes, too. At the Young Men's Christian Association, or YMCA, it was largely about saving souls. Sports programs there were largely driven by Muscular Christianity, the notion that a boy's spirituality was linked to his level of physical fitness. The more baskets he shot, the more committed the young athlete might be to a pious life. Likewise, the YWCA used sports to reach out to young women and girls. In 1884, the Boston branch opened the first YWCA gymnasium. In Buffalo, New York, in 1905, the local YWCA featured a swimming pool, one of the first in the country for women only. And the YWCA of Washington, D.C., boasted all-female badminton as early as 1932. Yet throughout the early twentieth century, organized sports for children were overwhelmingly organized sports for boys. Girls were considered too delicate. Who knew what harm could come to them shooting baskets or running track? They might develop muscles, certainly no advantage when the time came to find a husband. Some thought physical activity might even prevent girls from having their own children later in life. No joke. As late as the 1970s, Kathrine Switzer, the first woman to run in the Boston Marathon, claims she was confronted with the astonishing prediction that distance running might cause her uterus to fall out.

It was different for boys; boys were born to compete on the sports field and beyond. Every time they stepped onto a court they were honing skills that were necessary to succeed in what sports historian Allen Guttmann refers to as "the breadwinner's struggle." Not so for girls.

"While clouting a baseball and dribbling a soccer ball were thought to be a useful preparation for careers in industry and commerce, middle-class women were excluded from these branches of endeavor, and few mid-Victorian moralists imagined a connection between ballgames and childcare," Guttmann writes in *Women's Sports: A History*.

In the lives of boys, however, organized sports was more than training for an office job. America's cities increasingly looked upon them as a form of social engineering. "It's the football field, the diamond, the track against the party, the dance, the pool parlor, and the saloon," warned one New York state judge in 1909. The sentiment was shared by the archetypal outdoorsman of the day, Theodore Roosevelt. The former president argued that the way to cut the alarming rate of juvenile delinquency was to build more urban playgrounds. "The young criminals are created not by their school life, but by what is done in their leisure hours," the former president opined in 1926. "By striving for a proper opportunity from outdoor recreation...for all our boys and girls we will do a very great work toward cutting down crime."

The most successful youth sports programs resided in the public schools. In 1903, the first organized sports league for boys had its start in the schoolyards of New York City. The Public Schools Athletic League began with three hundred eager players. Seven years later, there were more than 150,000. The success of the school league was obvious in the numbers of both players and fans turning out for youth contests. Yet by the 1930s, educators had become concerned. The emphasis on winning was too great, they warned. And the physical and mental strain of playing for championships was unhealthy for the young players.

School sports programs were rethought and refocused. The old emphasis on competing and winning was replaced with the loftier goal of physical fitness for all students. Leagues withered and elementary schools and junior high schools dropped their competitive teams in favor of less competitive intramural sports. Into the void stepped parents. It was a profound moment and, argues sports historian Rainer Martens, "a gigantic blunder" on the part of educators.

"Ironically, educators suddenly found themselves no longer leading the movement they had begun. Instead of well-trained professionals guiding the sports programs of children, well-meaning but untrained volunteers assumed leadership roles. Sadly, educators were left on the sidelines shouting their unheeded warnings and criticisms," writes Martens in his seminal book *Joy and Sadness in Children's Sports*.

No question, parents brought with them a different mindset. Unencumbered by academic perspectives about the damage that intense sports could inflict on children, they set up leagues that dialed up the competition. One of the earliest was Junior Baseball, a creation of the American Legion launched in 1926. The legionnaires liked baseball well enough. But like adherents of Muscular Christianity before them, they had a greater goal in mind. In the years after World War I, they fretted about a crumbling of moral values among young people. They feared that someday the country would be turned over to a generation of weak-willed, apathetic adults unable to defend themselves against the worldwide scourge of Communism. The answer seemed obvious: baseball. They hoped the national pastime would promote patriotic values, sportsmanship, and fitness among teenage boys.

In 1929, the Junior Football Conference entered the picture. Later (and better) known as Pop Warner football, the league began as a crime-prevention program in a blighted section of northeast Philadelphia. It remained an obscure operation until 1934, when the legendary college football coach spoke at a league function and so impressed the audience that league officials renamed it after him.

The 1930s wasn't a particularly promising decade to start anything, much less anything as novel as Little League Baseball. The Great Depression gripped the country. In 1933, when economic times were hardest, just one in every ten or fifteen high school graduates could find a job. A quarter-million children had no homes and drifted around the country in the hope, often futile, of finding places to live and work, according to Steven Mintz in his book *Huck's Raft: A History of American Childhood.* Carl Stotz did not have an easy time feeding his family. In 1938, the year his Little League dream was taking form, he held four jobs, working at an oil company, as a landscaper, at a venetian blind manufacturer, and finally as a bookkeeper at a local lumberyard. Part of the year, he survived on the salary of his wife, Grayce, and his twice-monthly unemployment checks of $12.10.

In the spring of 1939, Stotz's Little League made its debut with teams, including one sponsored by a local pretzel company. The concept delighted the children and caught on with parents first in Williamsport and then elsewhere. Within a decade, Little Leagues were operating in twelve states. By 1952, Arthur Daley, the esteemed and generally circumspect sports columnist of the *New York Times,* was extolling Stotz's creation. In one syrupy column, he referred to Little League as "the biggest thing to happen to the sport since Abner Doubleday outlined his baseball diamond in Cooperstown in 1839."

Not everyone was impressed. Inside the ivy-covered walls of American universities, professionals in youth recreation were troubled—not just by Little League, but the rising tide of leagues like it. As University of Washington historian Jack W. Berryman writes, beginning in the 1930s, academics issued "a steady stream of proposals, guidelines, speeches, manuals and periodical articles containing warnings against too much competition for elementary school children."

Those concerns are remarkably unchanged from ones that frame the debate today: youth sports were too competitive. Talented players got all the glory; weaker ones rode the bench, never developing skills or self-esteem. In 1932, an article in the prestigious *Journal of Health and Physical Education* warned of another potential harm seemingly stolen from today's headlines: early sport specialization. "Not only does [premature specialization] deprive the young athlete of the opportunity to brouse [*sic*] around and find his interests in the various sports and various positions, but it causes him to lose his adaptability," wrote the journal's alarmed editor. "Many athletic misfits are created."

Little League just kept rolling on. In 1947, Stotz presided over the first Little League National Tournament, a modest precursor to the Little League World Series. As his league was gaining a national profile, so was he. As early as 1952, Stotz attended the annual National Baseball Hall of Fame induction ceremonies in Cooperstown, New York, mingling with the sports royalty there. And as the stature of Little League grew, he formed his own glittering guest lists to the

Williamsport tournament. Most years at least one baseball legend attended. In 1952, Stotz escorted his special friend Connie Mack, by then the elderly eminence of the Philadelphia A's. Three years later, Stotz's companions included two inductees to the Baseball Hall of Fame, Lefty Gomez and Cy Young.

Charles Bucher was appalled. The New York University professor knew well what little children needed from their sports activities. What Stotz was offering certainly wasn't it. Bucher's credentials were impeccable. A tall, trim professor in NYU's School of Education, and later a delegate to President Eisenhower's White House Conference on Physical Fitness, he was a deep thinker about early childhood development. He had studied the issue from numerous angles, having also been an elementary school coach and athletic director. Clearly, he'd hung around his share of gymnasiums and athletic fields. He played golf, tennis, and enjoyed jogging. He believed in exercising every day. Later in life, Bucher even won the national championships in seniors doubles platform tennis.

Bucher entered the national debate through a side door. On September 1, 1952, he opened the *New York Times* and spotted a brief article on the paper's editorial page. It ran just 135 words and likely brought smiles to the faces of most readers. A few days earlier, the Little League World Series had crowned as its new champion a team from Norwalk, Connecticut. The *Times* cheerily tipped its cap to the winners before concluding: "The Little League has become a fixture in American life—and a valuable one indeed."

Bucher didn't think so. He fired off a letter to the newspaper published seven days later under the headline "Limiting Boys' Sports: Emphasis on Competitive Game for Children Criticized." In his response, Bucher listed reason after reason why parents should be wary of Little League Baseball, then in its thirteenth season. To the professor, the entire enterprise was designed to please and entertain adults. Little about it struck him as right for adolescent boys.

Little League "is a highly organized competition and is climaxed by a World Series," Bucher wrote. "Are youngsters from 12 years of age sufficiently mature and emotionally stable to the point where they should be engaging in an experience which has the potentialities for traveling 2,000 miles to play a game of baseball before eight or nine thousand spectators?"

The idea that boys would concentrate on one sport also troubled Bucher. He wrote, "The period 8 to 12 years of age should be an exploratory period when youth should be playing many activities...This is not the time to specialize too intensively in one activity. The child at this age needs experiences which involve the use of the whole body." That viewpoint still reverberates in the youth sports debate today.

It was hardly Bucher's last word on the excesses of youth sports. In July 1953, the professor took aim again in a *Look* magazine article bluntly titled "Little League Baseball Can Hurt Your Boy." A highlight of Bucher's piece—or lowlight, depending on the youth sports leanings of the reader—was the litany of horror stories chronicling deplorable behavior of coaches and parents. One story was of a father in Bucher's neighborhood in Armonk, New York, who boasted to friends that one day his son would pitch in the big leagues: "He has sold the idea to the boy and to some of the neighbors too. Perhaps this boy will make it. But the odds are about 25,000 to 1 against him. When he discovers, as he probably will, that he is no budding Yankee or Dodger it may not do his ego much good. He may even feel he has let his father down."

Bucher was far from a lone voice and youth baseball was far from the only target of those questioning the role of adults in organizing sports for children. By the mid-1950s, a full-blown debate had broken out among academics, physicians, and plain old adults arguing thorny issues such as who should be in charge and how competitive games for children should be. By then, a panoply of new leagues and national tournaments had cropped up. Pop Warner and Little

League Baseball made room for Biddy Basketball, Pee Wee Hockey, and even Little Britches Rodeo, a competition for prepubescent cowboys that got its start in Littleton, Colorado, in 1952. In keeping with the times, all were for boys only.

The forty-six-page booklet was titled *Desirable Athletic Competition for Children.* The only thing dull about it was the title. On December 18, 1952, the National Education Association held a news conference in Washington, D.C., to discuss its new report, and a roomful of reporters showed up, including scribes from the Associated Press and the *New York Times.* Then, as now, what the NEA said about children mattered. Founded in 1857, the powerful and influential organization was a thoughtful leader in efforts to expand education and improve schools. Among its 3.2 million members today are elementary and secondary teachers, higher education faculty, and school administrators.

The NEA report was a double-spaced demolition of youth sports. It panned the entire enterprise, concluding that "highly organized competition, patterned after high school and college sports, gives youngsters an exaggerated idea of the importance of sports and may even be harmful to them." The report, which had taken three years to complete, urged adults to do away with "high-pressure elements" in their programs, including all-star teams and newspaper and radio accounts of games that included "individualized publicity about good players." It recommended a total ban on tackle football for children not yet in the ninth grade. In short, the NEA seemed to be telling the organizers of Pop Warner, Little League baseball, and other leagues to pack up their equipment and go home.

Bob Wolff remembers his reaction well. "I thought they were making a big deal about nothing." At the time, Wolff was one of the most prominent sports broadcasters around. Beginning in 1947, he had been the radio voice of the major league Washington Senators. In the next six years, he would be at the microphone for Don Larsen's World Series perfect game in 1956 and the Baltimore Colts' sudden-death victory over the New York Giants in 1958, the National League Football contest dubbed "The Greatest Game Ever Played." (At age eighty-seven, Wolff was still dabbling in broadcasting and writing a memoir.) In 1952, Wolff was also a staunch defender of bigtime youth sports, though he certainly hadn't planned to be. He'd read an article about a football bowl game for youth players in Lakeland, Florida, called the Santa Claus Bowl, and he inquired about bringing a team from Washington to play in the game. Soon Wolff was leading a campaign to raise the $3,300 needed to send twenty-five players to Florida. Publicizing the drive on his nightly radio show, Wolff recalls that the money was quickly raised. But the NEA report, released just seven days before kick-off, threatened to spoil the party. Wolff appeared on countless news programs defending the game and debunking the NEA. The day after Christmas, the game came off without a hitch, except that a number of the Washington boys came down with a stomach virus and spent the night before kick-off in a Lakeland hospital. Even that proved redemptive, though, because the boys met an elderly patient during their stay and, after winning the game, returned to the hospital to award him the game ball. Notes Wolff, "That was pretty good proof that those kids kept their balance."

With educators raising questions, youth sports organizations were under pressure to consider reform. There's little evidence that they responded. In 1954, Little League Baseball's president, Peter J. McGovern, appointed "a special three-man committee" to study the Little League World Series and recommend whether it should continue. "There has been some criticism of the Little League's national tournament...because of the pressure and strain on youngsters participating in the title competition," noted the *Sporting News* in a paragraph buried on page 36. Whether such a committee ever considered the issue isn't clear. A half century later, I can find no other references to the issue. By 1957 McGovern was ready to change the subject, telling a reporter, "As for our critics, we have the research with which to tell them, 'The charges you make just aren't so.'"

The national debate about the alleged shortcomings of youth sports waxed and waned, but during the 1950s it never went away. In 1956 President Eisenhower established the first President's Council on Youth Fitness and charged it with keeping the nation informed on issues pertaining to children and their sports lives. The first chairman was Eisenhower's vice president, Richard Nixon, suggesting that a deep knowledge of sports was not needed for the position. The council's early recommendation echoed themes from the NEA report. Namely, "Schools...should focus increased attention on children who are not athletically gifted, rather than on 'stars.'" In June 1958, attendees at the American Medical Association's annual meeting in San Francisco heard a similar rebuke of all "highly organized sports for children." Dr. Fred V. Hein, an AMA official, told the group that structured sports leagues "shut out" all girls as well as boys who were not physically gifted. The system of catering to the most talented players "helps to perpetuate physical unfitness among the rest of children," he said. It is a critique of youth sports that still holds. In local rec leagues, talented children and their less athletic teammates share the same bench. But marginal players often make do with less of the encouragement and praise that result in esteem-building. Thus, one in three children quits a sports team each year according to a prominent study, a distressing rate of attrition.

Damon Burton, a University of Idaho professor, has studied why kids abandon sports for years. He has a plan to address the problem. Burton recommends equalizing playing time for talented and not-so-talented players, and insisting that coaches rotate children through all positions instead of relegating the less gifted ones to the athletic hinterlands also known as right field. "The key is to allow all players to feel a part of the action and to contribute meaningfully to their team's success," writes Burton in his article "The Drop-out Dilemma in Youth Sports."

Stotz would have seconded that. In a cruel irony, the man

who literally invented youth baseball lost a power struggle with the corporate types he'd invited to help manage the growing organization. He was ousted from Little League in 1956. He stayed on in Williamsport until his death in 1992, but never attended another Little League game. The reason for the messy split was Stotz's alarm with Little League's distressingly big ambitions. For the last four decades of his life, he railed about it in print any chance he got, which was often.

In 1964, the *Los Angeles Times* published a four-part series on the growing pains of Little League Baseball, probing everything from dysfunctional parents to the alarming incidence of pitcher's elbow. The provocative stories, several of which ran on page 1, caused a stir. The most incendiary article in the series was one that featured Stotz, eight years after his ouster and as angry as ever.

"I discontinued my connection in 1955, when I saw the way things were going. The national organization with headquarters here [in Williamsport] began developing into a Frankenstein. I became utterly disgusted. Originally, I had envisioned baseball for youngsters strictly on the local level without national playoffs and World Series and all that stuff. I still have kids in Williamsport playing baseball but not as part of Little League Baseball Inc. with its paid officials and a full-time research director."

A loose, unofficial alliance of skeptics and dissenters was emerging: educators, physicians, a youth sports pioneer—and a major league baseball pitcher. For years, Little League Baseball pointed to Joey Jay for validation. As the first Little Leaguer (from Middletown, Connecticut) to graduate to the major leagues in 1953, Jay was living proof that the organization had, in a sense, arrived. Its former players now were grown men contributing to society and, in Jay's case, leading the Cincinnati Reds to the 1961 National League pennant. In 1965, Jay was a twenty-nine-year-old husband and father living in a Cincinnati suburb. He signed up his seven-year-old son to play in a Cincinnati Little League and was surprised to find neither his wife nor his child happy. "My wife kept complaining that Stephan was coming home tense and exhausted. I went to one game and watched angrily while the coach made a tired six-year-old who just couldn't get the ball over the plate go back to the mound and keep pitching until he was ready to collapse," Jay said.

Jay wasn't angry only about his son's experience. In 1966, *True* magazine published his article "Don't Trap Your Son in Little League Madness," which decried the state of Little League Baseball everywhere. The article was part commentary, part diatribe. It challenged the qualifications of coaches and the motives of parents. It questioned the health effects of Little League on young bodies. As Jay saw it, kids were far better off learning and enjoying sports on their own than being under the thumb of adult minders. "What happens today is that many Little Leaguers are burned out before maturity. I think this explains why Little League has had such limited impact on baseball, why it has failed to produce a gold mine of talent not only for the majors but for high schools and colleges as well. The fault lies in its concentration on immediate victories and premature glory, rather than on teaching basic skills and sound development...Championships seem to come first, the youngsters last."

He called out "idiotic fathers" who made being the star of a Little League squad "a new status symbol not far below a Cadillac convertible." Mothers were equally chastised for being caught up in the "Little Leaguer status race." Jay (or more likely, Jay's coauthor Lawrence Lader, with whom he shared a byline) wrote, "I saw one mother shout at her boy as he left the field after an error, 'Don't embarrass me again before everyone!' Mothers from opposing teams often trade insults in the stands over their sons' prowess. Neighbors end up feuding with each other...In their mania for victory, adults can wreck the whole concept of sportsmanship."

Jay was appalled by "how many coaches are frustrated athletes, hell-bent on producing winning teams to recreate their own dreams of vanished glory. Many fathers take over their teams and consciously or subconsciously push their sons' careers. Their driving ambition has produced a new medical ailment, 'Little League elbow.'" Jay's description was more caricature than anything else, but I knew from experience that the problem parents whom he described hadn't disappeared from the bleachers. My son had the damaged elbow to prove it.

Fifty years ago, Little League Baseball's founder knew something was dead wrong with the direction organized sports for children was taking—and he exposed it. So did a roster of college professors, professional educators, medical doctors, and at least one major league baseball pitcher. All were arguing their case before the American public in something like a howl. None could stomach the idea of kids programmed from the cradle to be sports stars with flawless backstrokes and untouchable fastballs. And they'd never even heard of Tiger Woods.

2 TIGER TRACKS

Karen Foster of Dallas, Texas, is a wife and mother of three young children. Her greatest joys are time spent with her family, playing golf, and thinking entrepreneurial thoughts. About six years ago, she dreamed up an entirely original business idea. The concept seemed in perfect pitch with the rising tide of interest in youth sports. Foster formed a company and called it athleticBaby.

The concept is simple, if somewhat startling. Produce a library of sports DVDs for young viewers—very young viewers. "We say three months and up," says Foster, a former corporate executive. There was no need to hire famous sports personalities to kick balls and swing clubs—the target audience is too young to recognize them. Likewise, no real dialogue is needed since some of Foster's customers are just learning to speak.

Foster says she started athleticBaby to help parents help their babies. She points out that a decline in physical activity among American children is alarming and that the country faces "monumental" issues with childhood obesity and type 2 diabetes. "Childhood inactivity is at an all-time high. That is a paramount concern to me," Foster says, though it seems fair to note that the marketing pitch on the DVD packaging is silent about these serious issues. The DVDs boxes carry the catchy phrase "Encouraging winners one at a time."

The full line of Foster's DVDs is available on her company's Web site, athleticbaby.com. Surf there and find the world's largest selection of sports titles for diaper-clad viewers including *athleticBaby Golf, athleticBaby Soccer,* and *athleticBaby Basketball,* a newborn's introduction to life on the hardwood. Like all of the DVDs in the athleticBaby lineup, it runs thirty minutes and sells for $16.99. The Web site pitch notes: "Little viewers will be encouraged to roll, bounce, dribble and toss while enjoying colorful and exciting images of basketball fun—kid style!"

With the infant sports DVD market locked up, Foster is looking to new ventures. Recently athleticBaby launched a six-stage sports and fitness program for infants and tots called Little Athletes. The company has even made its move into the toy market, with a signature line of plush playthings for babies and toddlers. Now every infant can pursue his or her own sports passion with a pillow-soft basketball hoop, golf-club set, and the like.

Foster is a bright, enterprising businesswoman; athleticBaby is bizarre. Who knew the world needed teaching aids for soccer players too young to stand and basketball tikes who dribble effortlessly on their bibs? While such products may be new, the notion that sports champions need to begin their training before the first day of nursery school is anything but. It roots can be traced back at least thirty years to a television studio outfitted with a makeshift putting green and driving range.

On October 6, 1978, Americans tuned their televisions to the *Mike Douglas Show* seeking ninety minutes of agreeable entertainment. Douglas, a daytime talk icon of the 1960s and '70s, did not disappoint. The amiable host delivered a star-laden lineup: Jimmy Stewart, the great actor, then seventy, and Bob Hope, the comedian still cracking one-liners at seventy-five. Near the end of the show, Douglas brought out a third guest, one not quite as tall as Stewart's pant leg and probably a few years younger than Hope's necktie.

"Right now," Douglas announced, "I'd like you to meet Tiger Woods and his father, Earl Woods." The band struck up a tune appropriate for *Sesame Street,* and the audience applauded politely. From behind the curtain, Tiger toddled onto the set, eyes wide, carrying a few clubs in a golf bag made by his mother, Tida. It was not the Tiger we know. This Tiger had a sweet, round face, framed by black curls. His voice was a squeak.

With his father's help, Tiger teed up a ball. Then, as Douglas and the others stood back, Tiger took a full back-swing and made solid contact, popping the ball ten feet in the air.

Kneeling beside his guest, Douglas asked, "How old are you, Tiger?"

Earl responded for his son.

"Two."

Tiger wasn't old enough to cross the street alone. Yet he was on the road to becoming one of the greatest athletes of his generation. Woods's precocious cameo on the *Douglas Show* was kitschy entertainment. Yet for the millions of parents watching—and tens of millions who have heard about it over the years—it sent a powerful message: it's possible to turn your kid into a champion if you start early enough.

Years later, countless American families are traveling the Tiger path, one they hope will lead to a college scholarship or perhaps the promised land of professional sports. If anything, they are starting earlier and investing more than Earl Woods ever dreamed of.

A few years ago, the age of entry in most rec leagues was seven or eight. This has dropped to four in many communities and, startling as it seems, eighteen months in others. The Lil' Kickers program, a national organization with affiliated leagues in many cities, is among those that see age as no object. Its programs, offering "movement activities" and "lots of goal kicking" begin with children not yet two. The bar can't go much lower—or can it? Bob Bigelow, a former professional basketball player and noted youth sports philosopher, wryly predicts that the next movement in youth sports will usher in "prenatal soccer." The players will be "padded pregnant women." Or what about an annual tee ball world series? (There really is such a thing, for kids seven and under, in Milton, Florida.)

For the driven parents who can shape their children into sports champions, the rewards are potentially great. The average salary of a National Basketball Association player in 2006 was an astounding $5.3 million. A college athlete who nabs a full scholarship to a private university, though not an instant millionaire, is cashing in as well. At Georgetown, a four-year full ride is worth about $190,000.

The odds against hitting that jackpot are impossibly long. And the challenges a child encounters along the way are enough to cause any responsible parent to stop and think. The scourge of early sport specialization is now upon us. Today's teenagers are pioneers in this dangerous experiment, opposed by many doctors, in which children play one sport year-round. And we live in an era of sport coaching and counseling on demand. A cottage industry of private trainers, tutors, and therapists has entered the picture, turning up performance a notch but also raising the price tag for playing sports. As expenses rise, so do a parent's expectations. Why pay top dollar for private goalie lessons only to see your kid ride the bench?

All these changes are dangerously lifting the temperature, contributing to a perverse global warming of youth sports. The rules of the game are the same. Yet the stakes seem so much higher. By the time she is nine, a child playing soccer in the neighborhood league is likely to be jockeying for a place on a travel team, the next level up the competition chain. To continue moving upward, she must improve her skills while making the other sacrifices expected of elite players.

There's never been a more confusing time to be the parent of a young athlete. As grownups, we talk a good game about what we expect from youth sports for ourselves and for our children. If our kids make friends, have fun, and pick up a few basic skills from their sport, it's been a good season for them and for us. The reality often is more complicated. Adults rely on youth sports to feed an array of our emotional needs. The frustrated jocks among us long to see our progeny succeed on the wrestling mat or diving board, where we never could. There's the affirmation that is attached to raising a namesake who is standout player. If a child is the most gifted athlete on the block, it stands to reason she was raised by the most gifted parents.

To earn that stamp of approval, we are investing in an ever-increasing array of sports training for our children. Sports summer camps are ubiquitous. (Ohio State's thriving football summer camp attracted more than four thousand campers a few years ago, some as young as ten.) Fitness companies promise increased agility with training programs tailored to a child's age, favorite sport, and even position. And for parents seeking that extra edge for their child, there is the brave new world of private instruction, sometimes under the tutelage of an ex–big leaguer.

Twenty years ago, the idea of scheduling an appointment to see the quarterback or goalie tutor would have been laughable. Now such entrepreneurs are as easy to find as piano teachers, though their fees are much steeper. Former New York Yankees slugger Steve Balboni opened the Steve Balboni Baseball School in Edison, New Jersey, where the affable, and no doubt knowledgeable, ex-ballplayer retools children's swings for $140 per hour. (The price includes Balboni posing for a photo with your child.) If you have to ask what quarterback guru Steve Clarkson charges to mentor your teenage football player, he's out of your price range. Clarkson, whose clients have included both of Joe Montana's teenage sons, bills $3,000 plus travel expenses for a talent evaluation. Hourly lessons start at $1,000.

Often, the clients of sports gurus are high school athletes

seeking to maintain an edge when their sport seasons end. But as the youth sports temperature nudges higher, some players are getting an early start—much earlier. A varsity field hockey coach at a major university says she is giving thirty-minute lessons to eight-year-olds after being approached by several families.

The benefits of such lessons to a child's development are real enough. In some cases, an experienced instructor can help a teenager tweak his skills and work with younger ones to instill a few basic fundamentals. Then there's the bond that can develop between a dedicated student and committed teacher. (When the teacher is a college coach, there's even a chance your child might end up on her recruiting list ten years later.)

Inevitably, though, a number of instructors say that problems arise when a parent can't accept that enough is enough. Former big league pitcher Jim Poole, who lives in the Atlanta area, a hotbed of youth baseball, typically advises parents to lay off pitching lessons for months at a time. "It's contrary to my interest. I'd be much better off" if adults signed up their children for tutoring year-round, says Poole, who charges $50 per half-hour session. But he's convinced that kids, especially those eleven to fifteen years old, need extended breaks. He estimates that 10 percent of the parents he meets ignore his advice completely.

Former big leaguer Tommy John is even more adamant. The ex-pitcher, immortalized by the elbow operation that bears his name, turns away all inquiries to work one-on-one with young children during much of the off-season. "I could give thirty lessons a week at one hundred dollars a lesson during the winter—just eight- to twelve-year-olds. I refuse to do it," he tells me. "Those kids do not need to be playing baseball year-round."

John's frustration with parents is palpable. "What they don't understand, and will never understand, unfortunately, is it makes no difference whether you start pitching at eight or eighteen. I can take a kid who has never pitched in his life until he's seventeen. By the time he's nineteen he'll throw as well as or better than the kid who's been pitching since he was eight—and have less wear and tear on his arm."

Still, our intuition tells us that if we want our children to live their (or our) dreams and play tennis at Stanford or basketball at Indiana University, time is of the essence. Training needs to begin now. Specializing in a sport is an advantage for a gifted child. After all, isn't that the lesson of Tiger Woods?

Not the right lesson. Consider what we can learn from listening to the athletes who *are* playing college sports. Each school year, Dr. John DiFiori interviews many of the incoming athletes at UCLA, where he is the attending physician for several intercollegiate sports teams. "When we do our incoming physical examinations, I will ask [players], how old were you when you specialized in your sport? The answer is usually much older than most parents think," he says. "It's not uncommon to hear, 'Well, I played soccer from eight to twelve, and I got tired of that and switched to volleyball.'"

Sport psychology researcher Lynn Pantuosco Hensch discovered a related point when she polled five hundred men and women college athletes from Division I and Division III programs. Pantuosco Hensch sought opinions about training in a single sport as preparation for playing in college. Nearly 65 percent replied that specializing before high school was not necessary to play in college.

Intellectually such information is difficult to dispute. Yet the urge to transform a child into a highly skilled, meticulously coached sports star often is irresistible. Dr. Joseph Chandler, an Atlanta orthopedic surgeon who has spoken out nationally about the epidemic of youth baseball injuries, notes this mindset is not limited to a few maladjusted moms and dads. Even those who appreciate the risks to adolescent arms of too much pitching, for instance, can be mesmerized as their ten-year-old has batters flailing and his strikeouts pile up. "We're all just tied up in the excitement of a kid winning a game. It's the most natural thing."

The excitement isn't even confined to the action on the field or in the pool. For adults, youth sports can become something of a social register. When a child is named to an elite or travel team there can be an unmistakable boost to an entire family's social standing. Dr. Lyle Micheli, one of the nation's foremost pediatric sports medicine physicians, notes that in sports families he has observed through the years the newfound attention can be disarming. "In a mobile society, if your child is on a travel team, you suddenly have thirty new people who are your best friends. You're going to barbecues with the soccer team and so on," Micheli says.

So much of what surrounds youth sports tempts and disarms us, distorting our judgment. One powerful example is ESPN, the twenty-four-hour sports cable network and cultural touchstone. With its fourteen TV networks, beaming every imaginable type of sports entertainment into homes around the globe all day every day, ESPN is tough to escape. Not that most of us are trying. Its precise impact on how adults perceive youth sports is unstudied and, for the most part, unknown. Yet there's little doubt that as the sports network extends its reach, the boundaries between pro sports and kids sports have become a blur.

ESPN seemingly draws no such distinctions. Courtesy of the network, professional basketball icon LeBron James made his debut on national TV while still a high school junior in Akron, Ohio. The 2002 game had all the trappings of a National Basketball Association megaproduction, from the broadcasters (Dick Vitale and Bill Walton) to the impressive audience. About 1.7 million homes tuned in, making the LeBron show the highest-rated program on ESPN2 in a year. "Obviously thanks to LeBron, it attracted a lot of attention," an ESPN spokesman stated—or understated—at the time. James was an old man compared to the eleven- and twelve-year-olds from the Little League World Series who perform each year on ESPN. In 2007, for the first time, the network telecast an incredible thirty-two games from Williamsport—the first time every inning of every game had been shown.

Sport psychologist Richard Ginsburg is one of many who are deeply troubled by the morphing of youth sports games into top-rated TV shows. The attention and pressure focused on Little Leaguers during the world series, in particular, he says, is "preposterous." "Adolescents sports aren't meant to be entertainment for adults," says Ginsburg, who treats youth athletes and their families at Boston's Massachusetts General Hospital. The stage is too big for kids so young, he says. And the experience can be especially cruel when, in front of millions, a child ballplayer lets a ball dribble through his legs, thus disappointing not only teammates but the hordes of adult fans hoping to return home as world champions. "A child that age can't differentiate their performance from who they are as a person. If I had a son playing at that level I'd have a real concern about protecting his childhood," he says.

Ginsburg is one of the truly provocative thinkers on the subject of youth sports today. His 2006 book, *Whose Game Is It, Anyway?,* coauthored with two Boston-area colleagues, is a trusty handbook for parents of young players, explaining not just why parents of young players should back off, but why for their children's sake they have to. Like a lot of health professionals, he's critical of pushy, overly invested grownups. Yet he distances himself from other critics by largely forgiving the parents. "Adults are not the problem. The culture is the problem," he says. In an interview, Ginsburg explains his theory, which is rooted in a curious irony: that the busier and more distracted adults are, the more attention they pay to their children's sports games. He contends that workaholic parents, hoping to compensate for sixty-hour workweeks, which distinguish them from their parents' generation, have become voracious consumers of material things, including the trappings of youth sports. They sign up for more leagues, nudge their children onto the most competitive travel teams, and lavish them with $150 lacrosse sticks and $100 swimsuits. "A lot of forces are pulling at parents. Because everyone is so damn busy, and the culture moves so fast, parents just get in line, without thinking why they're in line or what the line is about," says Ginsburg. "It takes a grounded parent who has thought about the issue thoroughly to step back and say, 'I'm not sure this is the right thing.'"

Millions of children manage to survive youth sports without emotional scars, despite the background din of contemporary American culture; their parents figured things out or they didn't, but either way the memories are mostly happy ones. Other families fall into traps, perpetuating the darkest and most troubling stereotypes about the obsessive behavior of adults. Dr. Eric Small, one of a handful of private practice physicians who specializes in treating children with sports injuries, notes that despair about playing a sport has been a factor in suicide attempts by two of his patients. In fact, teenage angst over wanting to quit a sport, but fearing the disappointment of a parent, is quite common. Dr. Lewis Yocum, the team physician of the Los Angeles Angels and surgeon of choice for hundreds of youth athletes each year, says he sees such cases frequently in his practice. In a typical situation, he says, a teenage patient comes to his office ostensibly to discuss a sports injury and a surgical option that can get him back to his team as soon as possible. When the young patient is alone with Yocum, he opens up, explaining he's ambivalent about the operation and uncertain whether to continue with his sport. His problem is that he can't face his parents. Yocum recalls the typical conversation with such a patient: "'Baseball is okay, but I like Susie and computers and other things. I don't know what to do because I don't want to disappoint my parents. It's *so* important to my dad.' If I have heard that once I have heard it a hundred times. There's no sense doing a big operation on those patients. There's a whole psychological quagmire for the kids to deal with."

Mary Raine, a sport psychology consultant in Mount

Kisco, New York, recalls a family who came to see her colleague Eric Small. The anxious mom and dad wanted the physician's advice about their son, a high school football player. The boy had taken a severe blow to the spleen and hadn't been able to return to the team. He'd come to consult with the doctor on when—or if—he would be able to play football again. After examining the patient, Small called the parents in for meeting with their son and explained that the injury had been quite serious, and that if the boy played football again he would risk being exposed to another blow, this one life-threatening.

The parents' reaction startled Raine. Rather than consider themselves lucky to snatch their son from the football field before something truly awful happened, they searched for ways to keep him in the game. As their son listened, they started negotiating with the doctor. Could their son play with a little padding around his waist? Okay, a lot of padding? "They didn't want to hear that he could not play football again," recalls Raine. "That was the most extreme case of denial we've encountered in fifteen years."

I shuddered as Raine shared that story of parents losing their common sense, mostly because it hit so close to home. My son Ben's spleen is fine, thank you. But when he was thirteen and a very fine baseball pitcher, a coach who should have known better inexplicably took liberties with his right shoulder. That reckless baseball coach was me.

Take what I have to say about my son's sports talent with the same grain of salt reserved for any proud parent. I feel safe in reporting that at that stage of his life he was an unusually eager and intense player. He was tall for his age, had more freckles than most and a shock of unruly red hair that always made it look as if there was a fire under his cap. As with most tall kids who think about nothing but baseball, his best position was pitcher. The rules of our community league allowed him to pitch three innings every game, and as coach and father, I felt an obligation to maximize this potential. (Translation: I wanted to win.) There was more at stake than trophies. Here I refer to vanity, and specifically to mine. I reveled in Ben's success in baseball for what it meant to him: new friends, self-esteem, an occasional mention in the local newspaper. I did not reject the reflected glory. That was *my* esteem-building. It's enormously fun to have a child who is a good player, one other parents notice and fuss about. I liked it when adults at the game would compliment him, unaware we were father and son. I'd allow the praise to wash over me like a morning shower. Then, as if speaking about an adolescent Mickey Mantle, I'd fess up to our shared DNA and remark demurely, "Ben loves the game." He was thirteen, playing on a neighborhood rec field. It was not Yankee Stadium. Yet for me his accomplishments felt like a pure and peculiar sort of validation, a weird kind of litmus test. My son throws strikes. Therefore, I must be a model parent. Yes?

One night, after a game late in the season, my sports parenting credentials were severely tested. Ben confided that his pitching arm, that prized right shoulder, did not feel quite right. It was a conversation I had never had before with my son. I sent him to school the next morning with instructions to find the athletic trainer and get his shoulder looked at. My mind was on my son's well-being—and on the league playoffs beginning later that week. This was no small issue (for me) because, though we had other able, eager boys and one girl on our team, we were likely going nowhere without a healthy Ben to hack through the heart of the opposing team's batting order. The next afternoon, after Ben had his brief consult, I dropped by the school to pick him up and sought out the athletic trainer, a responsible and highly professional young man named Dan. He explained that Ben appeared to have a mild case of shoulder tendonitis, an irritation of the tendon pretty much caused by one thing: throwing too many baseballs. No rush, but Ben should be examined by an orthopedic specialist, he explained. The doctor would make a formal diagnosis and counsel us as to how long Ben should lay off pitching, likely a few weeks to a month. I listened intently, hearing everything and understanding not a word. I say this because, in spite of the reasonable advice proffered, I ended the chat by asking the trainer: Can Ben pitch Friday?

It was an unusually dumb question given what had just been explained, even for a glory-seeker like me. I don't remember what the trainer said in reply. I can imagine what he must have been thinking. Perhaps, "Who is this lunatic?" True to the athletic trainer's oath, he was looking out for Ben's health. I, on the other hand, as the father of a thirteen-year-old passionate about baseball and relying on his dad's judgment, was focused on the playoffs. I didn't just inquire into Ben's fitness to pitch, I pitched him. Three days later, our ace was back on the mound with instructions from me to blaze a trail to the championship. I hadn't pushed him in front of a speeding car, nothing like that. But what I'd done was silly bordering on reckless and above all narcissistic. The irony of the situation was that if another mom or dad had used such terrible judgment at my son's expense, I would have been livid. As it was, I watched with regret and, in short order, remorse, as an injured boy attempting to please his dad lamely lobbed balls at home plate. After about a half-dozen throws, I walked out to the pitching mound and removed him from the game. He retrieved his bottle of Gatorade and took a swig, removed his cap, and watched for the rest of the evening from the bench behind the third-base foul line. Only one of us had anything to be disappointed about that evening. It surely wasn't Ben. On doctor's orders, he did not throw another baseball for eight weeks.

I had amazed and disturbed myself with the importance I'd attached to the outcome of a child's sports game. That hardly singled me out, I knew. We all want our children to succeed in whatever arenas they enter, tee ball or ballet. That response is perfectly normal, as sports psychologist Richard Ginsburg explained to me in one of the first interviews I conducted for this book.

"The question isn't whether we're emotionally invested in our children, because we are. It isn't whether we see ourselves in our children, because we do," he said. "It's when the investment becomes so great that what is good for the child is forgotten that real problems happen. When it becomes bragging rights or the parents finding meaning in their lives through the sports successes of their children, that's when you've entered the gray area." How is a parent supposed to recognize when she has wandered into that gray area? I asked. "The line is such a vague thing and it's different for everyone," Ginsburg said. "It's difficult. It always has been difficult. This isn't a new phenomenon. It's been going on as long as there have been children and parents, and there has been language to speak about it."

I was reminded of the remarkable investments that parents make to further the sports lives of children when I was introduced to Scott Albertson, who lives in Atlanta with his wife and four children. The oldest child, Anders, is one of the best fourteen-year-old golfers in his area, a hotshot featured on the Golf Channel and already being scouted by major colleges.

His family is sacrificing plenty to see that the young prodigy has everything he needs to keep lowering his scores. Sacrifices? Scott Albertson notes that his business has suffered from the days he leaves work early—or doesn't arrive at all—so he can walk fairways and stand on driving ranges with his son. He and his wife stopped buying clothes. They've never taken their kids on a vacation. When money was really tight, Albertson even skipped payments on his family's health insurance plan. "It came down to what we were going to do with that five hundred dollars: pay that or pay for golf." It's not all about Anders. The golfer's nine-year-old sister is on a similar journey as a competitive tennis player. Lessons and other expenses add up to another $100 a week, says her father.

The choices seem extreme, but not to Scott Albertson, who has borrowed liberally from the Earl Woods playbook.

Before his son was old enough to stand, Albertson recalls pressing a plastic golf club into his hand. He presented Anders with his first real set of clubs at age three.

From there, it's been onward and upward. At nine, Anders entered his first tournament and shot 113. A year later, in the same tournament, according to his father, he blazed a 73 and won. Of the first fifty tournaments the golfer competed in, he won thirty-nine. Now as a teen he spends his life hitting golf balls. His father says a typical summer day for Anders might be a round of golf followed by eight hours of practice at the driving range. *Eight hours.* "He has a work ethic unlike any kid I have ever seen," says his father. Such dedication has turned Anders into something of a youth sports icon in his hometown, where the acclaim even includes having been fodder for a current events quiz in the *Atlanta Journal-Constitution* in 2006.

> Q: Anders Albertson, 13, a student at Woodstock School, is a sensation in his favorite sport. What sport?
> A. Monopoly
> B. Golf
> C. Football
> D. Lacrosse

Scott Albertson says he spends $1,000 a month on golf equipment and entry fees and invests in his son's golf future in countless other ways for one reason: "Because it's what he wants to do." Albertson tells me, "I want him to take this as far as he wants to take it. Once or twice a month we sit down and review. I ask, 'Are you sure this is the route you want to travel? Is this what you continue to want to do?' It probably sounds off the wall, but if he decided to quit, my reaction would be 'Okay, fine.'" It does sound off the wall. With tens of thousands of dollars invested in full-throttle sports training, is it likely that a parent would allow a child to stop cold, no questions asked?

In the case of Anders Albertson, the point probably is moot. During a recent summer, at several tournaments, Anders's dad says his boy was trailed by college golf scouts. "We've heard from probably five Division I schools," Scott Albertson reports. At one event, a coach from a university with a highly competitive golf team followed Anders for thirty-six holes, says his father, who notices such things.

All in all, Scott Albertson is encouraged by his son's progress. "If he continues on, I feel certain he will be able to get a golf scholarship." That would be a credit to the perseverance of father, mother, and son. However, it might not be enough to balance the ledgers for all that the Albertsons have invested in their son's golfing career. For that, Anders will have to sink a few putts on the PGA Tour.

3   PARENTAL PAYOFF

It may be the worst part of Ray Reid's otherwise excellent job. Coaching college kids—very rewarding. Collecting soccer championships—what's not to love? The tough part of being a college coach is managing parents and their expectations for their children.

Reid is the respected men's soccer coach at the University of Connecticut, a squad that has won more than its share of Big East Conference titles and kicked its way to the NCAA championship in 2000. He's a bigtime coach of a bigtime college program and, as such, each year is socked with thousands of unsolicited letters, e-mails, résumés, and personalized DVDs from high school players, each pledging allegiance to UConn if Reid will utter the phrase *I want you*.

For almost all, the news will be disappointing. UConn has room to add only six to seven high school players each recruiting cycle, some years just four or five. Reid's sense is that teenagers often have an easier time accepting the bad news than their moms and dads, for whom a child's sports career has involved long years of driving carpool, pacing sidelines, and writing checks. These dutiful parents have done their part. Now it's payback time.

Reid bristles as he recalls conversations with parents for whom an athletic scholarship is expected, if not demanded. It goes this way, he says: " 'Coach Reid, we invested a lot of money in my son's career—thirty thousand dollars in ten years. We'd like a soccer scholarship to get some of it back.'

"It angers me. I'm appalled by the attitude. My reaction is: 'That's interesting. Your son is a mutual fund!' "

Reid's annoyance is understandable. (What coach—much less one who has notched a Division I national title—wants to tangle with moms and dads over a recruiting decision?) And, in a slightly perverse way, so are the inflated expectations of parents. After all, consider the road they have traveled with their children.

Early specialization boosts the soccer skills of eight-year-olds. Travel teams are a fast track for the most promising players to move ahead of other players their age. Summer sports camps break the routine of games and practices—with a daily routine of games and practices. Placement services lure parents with marketing pitches designed to sell a high school player's sports résumé like a pork belly future.

Some families are focused on athletics but not athletic scholarships for their sons and daughters. Instead, their hope is to leverage a sports talent into admission to a highly selective school, one that otherwise might be beyond a student's reach. In such cases, field hockey goalkeepers are selling themselves no differently than the star of the high school debate club or tuba players in the marching bands. They're all strutting their stuff for the admissions officer who might randomly open their file. "Even if your kid has [2400 SAT scores] and is president of her class, she still needs something else to make that college stop and go: *Hmmm*. Lacrosse for us has been that *hmmm*," says Joy Kirk, whose daughter, Chelsea, plays at Dartmouth, where there are no scholarships for athletes.

As Coach Reid tells us, other families are willing to spend big money precisely because they believe they are positioning themselves for a future dividend in the form of an athletic scholarship. No doubt, a percentage of moms and dads will be proven right. Their children will go on to play at the next level, having been wooed to their campuses with thousands of dollars in sports-playing money. But most will have been misled. They're in for a mighty letdown. Exactly how pervasive such outsized expectations have become is tough to say. But research shows many of us are living in this dreamland.

In 2006, Dr. Robert Rohloff, a Wisconsin pediatrician, surveyed 376 mothers and fathers of sports players, most in middle and elementary school, about their goals for their children's participation in sports. Almost 40 percent, a startling figure, told Rohloff they hoped their children would someday play for a college team. Twenty-two parents said they *expected* their children to become professional athletes. Even to someone who has never seen a tennis racket, that sort of optimism is wildly misguided. But how long are the odds? How daunting is the challenge to a young player hoping to make the jump from high school varsity to intercollegiate scholarship player?

Very daunting. Do the math, or consult the figures of the National Collegiate Athletic Association, which reports that, in many sports, fewer than seven high school players out of one hundred will move on. Just 5.8 percent of high school football players, one in seventeen, will suit up for a college squad. The odds are bleaker for men's soccer (5.7 percent), baseball (5.6 percent), women's basketball (3.1 percent), and men's basketball (2.9 percent). Of overall scholarship aid handed out to college students each year, sports awards are a sliver: 18 percent at public colleges and universities and just 7 percent at private ones, according to research by Sandy Baum of Skidmore College and Lucie Lapovsky of Mercy College, compiled for the College Board. In short, being a gifted biology major pays much better.

Even the students with the talent to land an athletic scholarship, in all but exceptional cases, are left with a tuition bill and sometimes a large one. With limited scholarships to offer, coaches carve up awards giving less money to more athletes. The average athletic scholarship for the 138,216 athletes in Division I or Division II schools in 2003–2004 was $10,409, about half the cost of attendance at some state universities and a fifth of tuition at pricier private ones. The best-compensated college athletes are the ones playing ice hockey. Both men and women players brought home, on average, 80 percent of full scholarships or slightly more than $20,000 per player. On the low end of the scale are sports such as volleyball, soccer, and, for men, wrestling. For their efforts, wrestlers who had earned athletic scholarships picked up just 37 percent of total tuition, a little more than $6,700, according to a *New York Times* report. One mother, whose daughter swims for the University of Delaware, offered this sobering appraisal to *Times* reporter Bill Pennington: "People run themselves ragged to play on three teams at once so they could always reach the next level. They're going to be disappointed when they learn that if they're very lucky, they will get a scholarship worth 15 percent of the $40,000 college bill. What's that? $6,000?"

Playing sports in college can be joyful and it can be a grind. At Division I schools it is unquestionably a full-time job. In 2007, the NCAA acknowledged as much, releasing a report that showed demands on athletes had risen sharply in recent years. Among the NCAA's findings: Many athletes spend as many hours practicing and playing their sports during off-seasons as when their teams normally play; and one in five college athletes told the researchers that their sports commitments had prevented them from choosing the major they wanted. Not a course. A *major.*

Francis Murray can relate. He is a bright, engaging college student who hopes to leave George Washington University ready to begin a career as an entrepreneur. This ambition has come only recently. For the first eighteen years of his life, Murray was under the spell of coaches who had shared their dream of playing baseball at a Division I school. "I dreamt of nothing else. I almost laugh when I look back at it," he says. "My goal wasn't to make money or own a business. My goal was to play baseball."

At a New Jersey high school famous for its highly competitive sports teams, Murray remembers receiving plenty of encouragement from coaches who were as interested in his pitching statistics as in his academic progress. "If I think about it, there were very few adults in my life in high school who were not coaches," he says now. He spent four years pitching for his high school team, buying into the dream of a college sports life that he says was promoted by the coaches around him. Then, when Division I coaches did not come forth with offers, he spent a fifth year honing his skills at the IMG Academies in Bradenton, Florida, the pricey boarding school for elite athletes. At the IMG campus, Murray was discovered by the GW baseball staff, which offered him a scholarship. He had realized his dream and was embarking on his college baseball career in the fall of 2006 when something unexpected occurred. Murray decided he did not want to be a college baseball player. In the end, the dream he had been chasing wasn't *his* dream.

Like a lot of teenagers, he'd grown up and out of his sports-playing ambition. The obsession was gone, replaced by interests in reading and his classes; in short, a life without sports. That, plus he had come face to face with the cold, hard reality of intercollegiate athletics. It's part lark, part grueling job. During the fall semester, baseball's off-season, Murray was expected to spend about four hours many days lifting weights and practicing with the team. He remembers standing on the baseball field during the early weeks of fall practice wondering how he got there and how to escape. "Every day, it felt more and more stupid. I kept asking myself, What am I doing wearing these pants and jacket? I should be doing my homework. I should be doing something beneficial to me down the road. I felt like a child out there. That's when the tipping point came."

He had not planned to quit the team. Yet one morning he found himself at the Museum of Natural History with a friend, enjoying the exhibits and determined not to cut short the visit even if it meant being late for practice. The next day, he met with the coach and quit. "I remember leaving there feeling liberated. Now my life was open. I could do whatever I wanted."

Murray didn't attend a single GW baseball game that first season. He didn't even pick up a baseball. Yet he's never been happier. "I suppose the lesson is that it's human nature to become obsessed with a dream," he says. "It's too bad when you pick the wrong dream."

The jockeying for college sports glory starts early. And it starts in places like the lush green athletic fields at Lewis University outside Chicago. On a sunny June afternoon, a few hundred children gather for tryouts for the Chicago Magic, possibly the most prestigious youth soccer club in the United States. The families who show up here are investing in more than the club's trademark white shirts and navy blue shorts and socks. They're investing in a child's soccer future.

John Hannan, the Magic's assistant director of coaching, confirms as much, telling me that unless a family has ambitious soccer goals, signing up for a high-achieving program like the Magic is "somewhat of a foolish investment. If you're not looking to play collegiately, or do not have goals beyond that, well..." Hannan's voice trails off for a moment before he adds, "This is a commitment!"

Commitment doesn't quite capture what's expected. Magic players, including those as young as eleven, are assumed to be dedicated to playing soccer year-round. Teams meet for practices or games four or five times a week, not including the high-profile tournaments where potent Magic squads show up in places like Dallas and Disney World. The parents who turn out for the tryout are braced for months of uninterrupted logistical challenges. The location of the Magic's austere headquarters, in a remote suburban strip mall, requires that many families commute with their children for up to an hour in each direction. Factor in rush-hour traffic in and around Chicago and there are afternoons when some players are spending more time getting to and from practice than actually playing soccer. The training, minus the gasoline, is about $450 for each of the Magic's three sessions per year, or roughly $1,400 a year. Uniforms, hotels, and meals on the road are extra.

Lourdes Sanchez isn't certain what she is paying for her son's soccer education and isn't that concerned. "I don't want to add it up—I'd be afraid," she says, only half joking. Yet she has no complaints. Her son, Rubin, ten, is an eager, bright-eyed player who is progressing rapidly under his Magic coaches. The feedback she is getting from those coaches is that her son, a center midfielder, has loads of talent and the right attitude to continue improving, just what she and her husband, a former professional soccer player, had hoped to hear. Like a lot of parents gathered at the edge of these soccer fields, walking their poodles and sipping McDonald's coffee, she has sports ambitions for her son. "I see him playing professional. I guess that's every parent's dream," Lourdes Sanchez says, and if not, then at least earning a college scholarship. The Sanchez family has more reason to hope than most, considering their son's drive and his father's sports background. Yet the odds against any high school athlete winding up on a professional sports team's roster should inspire no one—less than 1 percent for football and men's soccer players; less than .5 percent for men's ice hockey, baseball, and women's basketball players.

Even though Rubin Sanchez's soccer season has virtually no end now, it'll be even busier in a few years. By then he'll be a high school student and likely suiting up for that team too. The challenge of playing both club and high school teams is one of the new, hectic realities of youth sports. Kids want to play for their high school teams as a measure of loyalty to their friends in homeroom. They have to play for elite club teams to flag the attention of college coaches like Dave

Clarke, the women's soccer coach at Quinnipiac University in Hamden, Connecticut, who says he "totally ignores" high school soccer. Only players who thrive in the high-octane environment of club soccer, Clarke says, can play at the level he requires.

If they are the ideal proving ground for future college players, though, youth club sports teams are not risk-free. Few have thought as carefully about the dangers they pose as Al Scates, the legendary men's volleyball coach at UCLA, one of the nation's premier collegiate programs, for more than forty years. He's the winningest volleyball coach in the history of the NCAA and, with nineteen NCAA championships, shares the record for the most titles by a coach in a single sport. Scates knows volleyball and he knows volleyball players.

When Scates became the coach at UCLA in 1963, for the next few decades, he brought into his program nice kids, excellent all-around athletes. They seldom were students of volleyball. "In the old days, I was teaching kids who played basketball how to play volleyball," the longtime coach recalls. College athletes of that era, Scates says, also were a relatively healthy bunch. His teams could go months without a twist or strain and years between injuries that needed the attention of a surgeon. "Once in a while we'd see a sprained ankle. That's it," the coach says.

Flash ahead forty years to the golden age of specialization and club sports. Players joining the UCLA team have been locked in nearly year-round volleyball training throughout high school, sometimes longer. All those hours polishing skills have turned them into dynamite players. That's the good news. The bad is that they're orthopedic time bombs. "We're seeing kids with two knee operations before they even get to our program," Scates says. One of his starting players had ACL surgery on both legs as a high school player. Another, an all-American spiker, nearly had his career at UCLA interrupted by an overused shoulder. By the end of his sophomore season, the player's joint had become so lax that dislocations were common. A delicate operation on his shoulder put him back on the court.

Scates believes that young athletes are being disserved by year-round training. Listening to him, you get the impression that if elite clubs simply vanished from the earth he wouldn't mind. Yet Scates is quick to acknowledge that, like other coaches, he helps perpetuate an imperfect, even dangerous, system. Where does he find virtually all future UCLA volleyball players? Playing for elite clubs, of course.

Year-round training is raising concern in many sports. Major leaguer Tommy John tells of a conversation with former University of Hawaii baseball coach Les Murakami, a revered figure. During his thirty-one years as Hawaii's coach, Murakami had the best teams in college baseball. He had the pick of top high school players in the country. As John recalls, Murakami told him that though he could find pitchers for his team in talent-rich areas where baseball is played all year, he preferred to scout for players in "Northern climates." When John asked why, Murakami explained, "In Southern California, kids pitch twelve months a year. By the time they come here to go to college, they're either hurt or worn down."

We are on a mission to give our children access to the best coaches, the most intense training—when necessary, even the best lawyers. Sometimes protecting a young player's future means litigation. Case in point: a federal lawsuit known as *Rutherford v. Cypress-Fairbanks Independent School District,* which came to my attention thanks to an entertaining article in the *Virginia Sports and Entertainment Law Journal* by Timothy Liam Epstein. This case, like others Epstein cites, falls under the general heading of "disappointment lawsuits," an obscure if fascinating legal genre in which young athletes and their parents seek redress for damage inflicted to their sports reputations and college prospects. Players and their families almost always lose—Epstein does not cite a single winning case—yet it must be good therapy to argue the matter in court.

The Rutherford case, like most, was offbeat and doomed

to failure. The plaintiff, a senior at a Texas high school and a star pitcher, had used a student publication to lampoon two school coaches, a sin not forgiven by the Cypress High baseball coach, Archie Hayes. Judging Rutherford's comments as "unsportsmanlike, disruptive, demoralizing, and disrespectful," the coach informed Rutherford that he was being benched for Cypress's next game, a regional quarter-final playoff that Rutherford had been scheduled to pitch. Learning that their son had been scratched from the lineup, Rutherford's parents filed their lawsuit alleging a violation of due process under the Texas constitution.

The Rutherfords' legal case fizzled quickly. The presiding judge awarded summary judgment to the defendants, noting, "In every high school baseball game played in this nation each season, only one player may be designated the starting pitcher for a team, and that usually means that one or more other aspiring pitchers are relegated to the bench, to suffer the same disappointment as Kyle Rutherford. . . . The courts should not get involved in second guessing a coach's decision to play one person over another. Federal judges issue opinions and orders, not starting lineups."

The Rutherford case may sound like a classic waste of judicial resources. But as a trivial dispute it has a rival in *Wellsville-Middleton School District v. Miles,* which really was two frivolous state court cases. In the first, the school district sued the Missouri State High School Activities Association, claiming that its basketball team suffered an unjust defeat because the official scorer made a mistake. (The claim was dismissed by the court.) In the second, three aggrieved players from the losing team sued the referee. By failing to follow proper procedures in running the game, they argued that the referee harmed their chances of getting college scholarships. That suit was dropped after the first one was dismissed.

It's unclear from the court record whether the Rutherfords feared the coach's punishment tarnished their son's reputation with college talent scouts. In the case of an aggrieved Levittown, Pennsylvania, softball player, there wasn't a shred of doubt. In 2001, nineteen-year-old Cheryl Reeves filed a $700,000 lawsuit against her club softball coach, alleging that his "incorrect" teaching style had ruined her chances to earn a college athletic scholarship. Reeves argued that her personal softball tutor charged $40 an hour to teach an "illegal pitching technique" and that when she complained, the instructor, who doubled as coach of her elite club team, replaced her with his favorite players. Reeves says she was gripped by stress and forced to quit the team, unfairly ending her career as an elite player.

Few parents resort to such lawsuits to preserve a child's career in college sports. More stick to the tried, true, and labor-intensive methods of spending time and money to keep their children on course to play goalie at William & Mary or spiker at Pepperdine. Club sports are essential, of course. There's also an argument for the college sports matchmaker or, as youth sports advocate Bob Bigelow calls them, the "body brokers." Few companies offering such services existed even ten years ago. Now they're plentiful. Usually started by hustling entrepreneurs with backgrounds in sports, these firms pledge to carefully study your child's sports talents and, tapping into a vast network of collegiate contacts, match them with a university that just happens to be searching for a 200-meter breast-stroker or a scrappy wrestler in the 157-pound category. Normally the body brokers make calls to college coaches, produce flattering DVDs that display a player's strongest attributes, and then follow up until a scholarship deal is sealed (sometimes) or their overtures have been ignored by an indifferent coach (more often).

The quality of such assistance varies greatly depending on the outfit you're dealing with. Because they're totally unregulated, college sports placement services are free to promise and at times overpromise, giving the entire industry a Wild West sense about it. One firm, the Chicago-based National Collegiate Scouting Association, blows its horn with notable force. NCSA refers to itself as "the national leader in collegiate scouting" and its snappy, eye-pleasing Web site once displayed a marketing brochure that made amazing claims. According to the company, 95 percent of collegiate athletic programs use NCSA; the company's successful placement rate is 96 percent; and the average annual award for those using NCSA's services is more than triple that of students who opt for the do-it-yourself method of hunting for athletic scholarships: $4,345 to $14,511.

It seems too good to be true, and might be. Many of the NCSA's claims are anchored to statistics that are not independently verifiable. Others come from a report issued by the National Collegiate Athletic Association, the dominant governing body of college sports, which disputes the placement company's conclusions. "There is not any way that someone could take [NCAA] data and do an accurate assessment" of the company's value to individual students, an NCAA spokesman told me. I then spoke with an official of the placement company who stood by its conclusions. (Though the unconfirmed information has been stricken from the NCSA Web site.)

A respected outfit is the Baseball Factory, run by a couple of ex–Ivy League baseball players, Steve Sclafani and Rob Naddelman. Both men are known by a web of college baseball coaches across the country; one coach at a rigorous academic school with a nationally ranked baseball team tells me he pays extra attention to players recommended by the duo. And they have developed another talent at least as important in their business: managing the egos and inflated expectations of the anxious parents who walk through their front door. Most are reasonable people, they say. But you don't deal with as many moms and dads as Naddelman and Sclafani without running into some for whom a child playing highly competitive college baseball is a matter of great importance.

"We call it Division I-itis," says Naddelman. "Some families get very wrapped up in a child going to [college baseball powers like] Stanford or [the University of] Miami. Being able to say that in a local community defines some families. It can be interesting when a son gets hurt and that whole thing stops. Families don't know how to react. It's like somebody cut off their leg."

At our house, the age of enlightenment began when Ben was a high school junior, just a couple years after my regrettable move to ignore his sore shoulder. He was a good, not great, player for a small private school where the emphasis on sports was slightly overshadowed by the emphasis on AP history and accelerated chemistry. In short, he was not a shoo-in to play college sports.

My understanding of what it took to succeed as a collegiate baseball player was somewhat dated. Thirty years earlier, I had attended a half dozen practices for the freshman baseball team at my college. I was the only lefthander among the pitching hopefuls. For that reason alone, my prospects to make the team seemed bright, until one disastrous afternoon when a local community college visited campus for a preseason scrimmage. I was the starting pitcher and, in this key audition, gripped with one of the worst streaks of wildness ever seen. With an assortment of misfires, I walked each of the first six batters and then topped things off by hitting the seventh batter in the left kneecap. The humiliation lasted not even fifteen minutes. After the game, I neatly folded my double-knit uniform and returned it to the equipment manager. The next day I signed up to be a reporter for the *Daily Pennsylvanian*.

The idea that Ben might follow in my footsteps, though not too closely, had been playing on my mind for several seasons. He lacked the speed of a natural athlete. But by now he stood six-foot-three, was big and strong, and a very capable player. I was proud of him. I wanted someone, anyone, to tell me that he had a chance to play college ball. One fine May afternoon, I found somebody. His name was Al. I met him behind the backstop at the high school field where Ben's game was underway. Al was a gregarious man wearing a polo shirt. A longtime amateur baseball coach, he'd started a college baseball placement office with the name MVP or all-star or something similarly reassuring in the title. Al was representing a number of promising high school kids in the area, including the two best athletes on Ben's team.

I was hooked on a dream and hopelessly vulnerable. Al was a good salesman. For a small fee, $150 or so, he would meet with Ben to evaluate his baseball skills and discuss his college preferences. If Al felt that Ben was a bona fide college prospect, he'd recommend other steps and request more money. I wrote the check and was ready to write another.

Looking back, I see that Al and I were exceedingly well matched. From the start, he was reluctant to tell me that Ben was likely not college baseball material. And I was equally reluctant to accept such a gloomy verdict no matter how many times others—his summer league coach, politely, yet repeatedly—shared this same view. Ben and I spent the better part of a summer chasing this shared dream—signing up for showcase events recommended by Al at which we paid a few hundred bucks for his chance to audition an inning or two, preparing a Ben Hyman baseball video résumé, and visiting college coaches in their campus offices from Lexington, Virginia, to Williamstown, Massachusetts. Then, when we were both exhausted, Ben announced a clever change in strategy. He was refocusing his search on colleges where he thought he'd be happiest with or without a baseball team to play on. Once he settled in on campus, he might go out for the team as a walk-on and take his chances.

I should have been relieved. Ben was focusing on academics, which, after all, had been my responsible-parent mantra all along. Stacks of course catalogs started appearing in his room. And for the first time it seemed, we were having serious discussions not about whether some college baseball team played spring games in Tempe, Arizona, but about what his major might be. Perfect. So what about the situation did I find so utterly deflating?

4   EQUAL TIME

The college search might have gone differently if I had been flitting from campus to campus with a sports-minded daughter. But, tellingly, not so different anymore. For years, women were consigned to the margins of college athletics, expected to make do with less of everything. The times are rapidly changing. Nearly four decades after the enactment of Title IX, the law that effectively bars sex discrimination in school-sponsored sports, women have made major gains. If they haven't achieved equality with male athletes, they're closing in. Of athletes who competed in Division I college sports in 1990, 31 percent were women. That figure climbed to 45 percent by 2005. High school sports have witnessed a similar surge. The year Title IX took effect, 1972, boys playing high school sports outnumbered girls by twelve to one. Twenty years later, the edge had shrunk to fewer than three boys for every girl. The latest statistics from the National Federation of State High School Associations show girls comprising about 40 percent of high school athletes. Special congratulations go out to girl soccer players at high schools in Colorado, Hawaii, and North Dakota. In 2006, you outnumbered the boys.

The good news is that girls are catching up. But it's not all good news. As participation rises, so have influences transforming their games in troubling ways. Little girls now start on organized teams earlier than ever. In other words, as early as little boys. They're specializing in a single sport as middleschoolers. They're being courted by year-round travel teams, trained by private coaches, and sent to sports summer camps where the goal is college placement. (One rowing camp advertises a regular activity called College Recruiting 101.) For these fundamental changes, all credit goes to Title IX.

Title IX of the Education Act of 1972 changed everything for women playing sports. Congress passed Title IX as an amendment to the Higher Education Act with a straightforward intent: "No person...shall on the basis of sex, be excluded from participation in, be denied the benefits of, or be subjected to discrimination under any educational programs or activities receiving federal financial assistance." The act for the first time mandated "equitable" opportunities for women, but exactly what did that mean? Football teams for girls? Girls and boys basketball teams outfitted in unisex uniforms? Not that. But it would be years before the meaning of the act was fully teased out.

Title IX was not the beginning of sports for women, of course. Wimbledon crowned its first women's tennis champion in 1884. The first rulebook of women's basketball was published in 1892. And the U.S. Golf Association opened its gates to ladies just a few years later, sponsoring the first U.S. Women's Amateur Championship in 1895. Women in these competitions were swimming against the cultural tide of the day. As Welch Suggs explains in *A Place on the Team: The Triumph and Tragedy of Title IX,* "Two powerful social prejudices kept women from participating intensely in any sport or physical activity alongside their brothers. First, upper-class women were expected to be pale and dainty, and they often wore clothing like corsets that prevented them from breathing, much less running or jumping.... Second, a woman's primary functions in society were to attract a man and bear children and participating in sport was thought to impair the ability to do either."

The unenlightened were not only coaches. Women faced the same bias when they took their grievances to the courthouse. Court decisions keeping them off teams and out of competitions persisted almost until the day of Title IX's enactment. In 1971, teenager Susan Hollander sued her local school board because she was denied a chance to join the boys cross-country team at her Hamden, Connecticut, high school (there wasn't a girls team). Not only was she shot down, but the presiding judge offered this dubious explanation: "Athletic competition builds character in our boys. We do not need that kind of character in our girls." About the same time, a superior court judge in Asbury Park, New Jersey, ruled that a girl did not have the right to join the high school boys tennis team simply because there was no tennis team for girls. With the passage of Title IX, such jurisprudence quickly was consigned to the past. By 1973, a federal appeals court was taking a radically different view. As historian Allen Guttmann notes, the court ruled that high school girls in Michigan did have the right to try out for the boys tennis team even if they had the option of playing for a girls team.

Colleges and universities continue to grapple with Title IX. Over time, a plethora of court rulings have offered schools three ways to comply with the act: 1) Show similar rates of participation for men and women athletes; 2) have a history of growing sports opportunities for women and a strategy for expanding still further; and 3) prove that women are completely happy with the sports choices offered.

Rarely does a school with a suspect record even bother with option three. That leaves a complicated choice, especially for schools struggling to pay athletic department bills (which means virtually every school in the nation). Some address the imbalance by creating several new women's teams in, say, crew or fencing. As women enter the athletic pool, the overall gender ratio comes into balance. That was the approach at Vanderbilt, an academically rigorous institution best known in athletics for nationally ranked men's basketball and baseball teams. In 2005, Vanderbilt welcomed a new intercollegiate squad—women's bowling. Three years later, in a testament to the upward mobility still possible in women's athletics, the squad won the NCAA championship. The reverse approach is to eliminate men's sports teams, a move that inevitably stirs controversy on campus and riles alumni. In 2006, James Madison University met its Title IX obligation by eliminating ten of the school's twenty-eight sports teams, including seven for men. Parents of the athletes who lost their teams threatened a lawsuit. And a group of male swimmers started a protest Web site.

Despite widespread gains for women, double standards remain. The Women's Sports Foundation notes that women receive 45 percent of collegiate sports scholarship dollars to 55 percent for men. Women's sports also receive an even smaller share of the dollars that athletic departments spend on recruitment. Women seeking college coaching positions also continue to receive not-quite equal treatment, as any who has been in the job market recently can attest. Women coaches do not yet fill even 50 percent of coaching positions for *women's* college teams. And, on average, those in Division I earned 40 percent less than male coaches. A few female coaches are just now are crashing the green ceiling, led by University of Tennessee Lady Vols basketball coach Pat Summitt. In 2006, after thirty-one years, six national championships, and 913 games, UT rewarded Summitt with the first $1 million salary for a woman college coach.

Title IX has created a world of opportunity for girls. But as the stakes have increased, so have the choices and the challenges presented to parents. How young is too young for a child to get serious about sports? How many hours of training each day are too many? And what sacrifices are reasonable to help a child achieve the goal of a college scholarship or even a shot at becoming a professional athlete? In short, the same issues facing the parents of boys. Millions of families are struggling to find the proper path.

When I spoke to Ross Reeves of Euless, Texas, he was driving his fourteen-year-old daughter, Natalie, to a golf course where she would spend the day. It was hardly rare for Ross and Natalie to be traveling either to a golf course or from one. We spoke in July, the heart of the golf season. As Ross explained, his daughter had a golf club in her hand seven days a week. Some days, she'd play a four-hour practice round. On others, she'd practice for five hours. It's not just Natalie against the world. Each week, she spends time with her golf coach and a fitness trainer. All told, Ross estimated that he and his wife were spending $12,000 a year on his daughter's golf training. The hard work clearly is paying off. I received evidence by e-mail: an impressive golf CV listing Natalie's high school stroke average (74.8), round-by-round scores from twenty-three tournaments, and links to articles in Texas newspapers about her stellar play. "She obviously has talent," Ross told me. "She hits the ball farther than any girl I've ever seen, two hundred seventy-five to two hundred eighty yards."

The day after we spoke, Ross sent an e-mail continuing the conversation. As with many of the parents I spoke with, we'd spent a good amount of time discussing why he was so completely committed to Natalie's golf and to his younger daughter's interest in soccer. Clearly, he thought there was more to add. "I have been asked if I do it so my kid gets a scholarship. The answer to that is no. First, both my kids have college paid for if they need it. Second, if I saved the money I was spending on golf and soccer, I would easily have enough to pay for their college. I'm not sure about the answer of 'why' now that I think about it. Both my kids like competing and I love watching them play."

The why was evident when I spoke to Chinney McGee of Flint, Michigan. McGee's daughter, Dynasty, is one of the nation's most promising track athletes. Chinney started her in racing shoes when she was four years old. In 2007, as an eighth grader, she set a Michigan indoor track record in the 400-meter, running 56.02 seconds in a meet against high school athletes. The same year she set two AAU youth national records in the 200-meter (26.38 seconds) and the 400-meter (57.48 seconds). Chinney McGee coaches Dynasty and another daughter, Chyna, a pentathlete, and twenty other kids in Flint. They meet four days a week on the track at Flint High School, training after school from six to eight o'clock. The team calls itself the Flint All-Star Track Club, FAST for short, and travels all over the country competing in meets. In 2007 alone, McGee and his wife were on the road sixty to seventy days with their track prodigies, fitting in trips around Chinney's day job at UPS. As father and coach, Chinney's pride in Dynasty is evident. He revels in her progress and in her growing celebrity (including the ultimate validation for youth athletes: inclusion in *Sports Illustrated*'s "Faces in the Crowd"). He has other motives, too, like helping these children escape Flint, a place McGee alternately refers to as "America's poorest city" and a place with the third-highest crime rate in America. Or, an escape at least from the worst the city has to offer. That is what sports did for Chinney McGee when he was young. If not for sports "there's no way I would have gotten out. The only alternative would have been selling drugs," he told me.

Even as an eighth grader, Dynasty had sprinted down a path that is taking her far away from that life. Her track success is already turning the heads of college track coaches. If she keeps running and keeps studying, she will have scholarship offers from many schools. (Among her credentials as a middle school student, notes her dad, is a perfect 4.0 grade point average.) An athletic scholarship is Chinney McGee's goal for his daughter, though not his only one. "Track and field is extremely competitive. That will carry on in her life. She understands now that it's going to take hard work to get anything. The harder you work, the more success you have."

Natalie and Dynasty represent the third generation of Title IX athletes. Possibly the fourth. Before them were girls who are now grown women, some with their own children. How do they feel about the choices that adults who enabled their sports lives made for them? I asked a gymnastics legend. Her name is Torrance York, though her fans knew her as A Very Young Gymnast. In 1976, Torrance York was ten years old, a promising gymnast who trained five times a week with her school team in New York City. She was also a minicelebrity with an offbeat list of television credits, including guest shots on *Romper Room* and *The Merv Griffin Show*. Torrance's fame stemmed from the publication of a book of photographs and text called *A Very Young Gymnast*. Jill Krementz, the renowned photographer, had come up with the concept to follow a child athlete through her daily routine, snapping candid pictures all the way. The accompanying words were in the voice of the child, giving the books (earlier Krementz had published similar books about a rider, a dancer, and a skater) an intimate feel. "Gymnastics is so much fun!" That is the opening sentence of *A Very Young Gymnast*. The words appear under a photo of a pint-size Torrance poised on a balance beam, arms outstretched, legs in an impressive split. Her smile is so joyful it seems to occupy half her face. For the next 127 pages, readers followed Torrance to her Manhattan apartment, to school, and in one curious editorial decision, into the office of Dr. Friedman at Lenox Hill Hospital, where the little girl is pictured on an examining table in just her underwear.

At ten, a very young gymnast was a very full-time gymnast. After school every afternoon, she'd head for the gym to a practice that usually lasted two and half to three hours. Then, three nights a week, after a quick dinner in the locker room or the car, she'd dash to a gymnastics club on Long Island for another two-hour workout. There were gymnastic meets—twenty-eight the year the book came out. And one morning a week, before school, there were ballet lessons. It was a disciplined life for a child so young, Torrance York remembers. Her commitment to gymnastics required that she think in ways other children never did. She recalls being on a balance beam or parallel bars and having a stern inner conversation about what she would have to sacrifice if she did not perform a routine to her standards—"calling a friend or having dessert." The routine of practices and meets became so ingrained that even a free afternoon could leave the little girl feeling lonely and sometimes depressed. Torrance recalls, "I remember on weekends that I did not have a meet wondering, What do I do with myself?"

Torrance credits her mother for keeping her life somewhat in balance. After the book was published, Torrance had a chance to step up her training by attending a prestigious gymnastics academy that was a proving ground for future Olympians. To accept, she would have had to move away from home. She opted not to go, partly because her mom told her she didn't have to. "My mother always had a theory that my being in the book, that was one reason I allowed myself not to pursue the Olympic goal. I felt recognition in a different way." She continued in gymnastics on a less frenetic path, eventually competing for the gymnastics team at Yale. Now she is a mother of two young children and an accomplished photographer whose images have been displayed in museums and featured in solo exhibitions.

On August 16, 2008, the world's greatest Olympian stood poolside at the Beijing Olympics, fist-pumping like Muhammad Ali in a swim cap. Michael Phelps had just won another gold medal at the Beijing Summer Olympics. For those who were counting—and everyone was—it was Michael's eighth of the Summer Games, breaking Mark Spitz's record of seven gold medals in a single Olympics, which had stood thirty-six years.

Michael wasn't the only Phelps celebrating that day. In the stands, cheering and crying, was a special threesome—Michael's mother, Debbie, and older sisters Hilary and Whitney.

It made sense that the Phelps sisters would be nearby

when Michael entered the record books: They were first in the pool. Before Michael could read, Hilary was an accomplished swimmer tearing up the competition in local meets back home in Maryland. (She'd later go on to swim at the University of Richmond.) Next came Whitney, five years older than Michael. When he was just a scrawny kid, she was already a powerhouse.

By all accounts, including her mom's, Whitney loved competitive swimming with a passion unmatched by other kids. She was tireless, relentless, and a natural. Hilary was terrific, too. But back in the 1990s, Whitney was the swimmer named Phelps that people had their eye on. No one expected more of Whitney than she demanded of herself. From the moment she won her first race as an eight-year-old, her aim was to be an Olympic champ, and two adults were there to help her live her dream. The first was mom, of course.

As a sports parent, it's tough to beat the credentials of Debbie Phelps. A middle school principal, and a nurturer by nature, she hardly began with a plan to train any of her children into Olympians. The main attraction in getting her kids started in swimming was water safety. She wanted them to conquer their fears early in life. Years before Bob Costas was interviewing her in Beijing, she lived a swim mom's anonymous and harried existence, volunteering at meets, shuttling to practices at all hours, always on call when her kids needed this or that.

Murray Stephens is a coach who seems to own the Olympic rings. For years, the acclaimed swim teacher watched over Whitney's progress in the pool—and that of hundreds of other aspiring Olympic freestylers, breast-strokers, and the like. From Meadowbrook Swim Club, his unassuming headquarters below the Kelly Avenue Bridge, Stephens molded several generations of champions as he built one of the most formidable programs in the country. A gallery of the club's past and present Olympians fills a wall overlooking the club's six-lane, fifty-meter indoor pool. Michael is the only swimmer whose photo hangs on the wall twice.

Whitney, unbelievably for those who can recall her effort-lessly cutting through the water, is missing from that wall. She had the goods. She was tough and determined and hugely talented. In 1994, as a thirteen-year-old, she qualified for her first World Swim Championships. A year later, Whitney was the U.S. national champion in the 200-meter butterfly. Her career on the ascent, by age fourteen, she ranked first in the United States and third in the world in her best event. She was considered an odds-on favorite to be not only a member of the 1996 U.S. Olympic team but also a stalwart, a star. But it did not happen. Instead, something shocking occurred at the U.S. swimming trials. Needing to finish in the top three in her event to punch her ticket to the Summer Games, she came in a disappointing sixth.

Whitney kept swimming. But at sixteen, her glory days were behind her. She never competed in the Olympic trials again, and though she went on to swim for two years in col-lege, she was never anything close to the unstoppable stroke machine she had been as a kid swimmer.

What happened? Her body rebelled. In fact, she tells me, it had been rebelling for years before her swim life came un-hinged at the Olympic trials. The signals had been there for a very long time. She was too young, distracted, and driven to interpret them. The adults around her failed to read the situ-ation correctly, or at all. Whitney vividly remembers swim-ming through pain in her back at age ten. She recalls pains so intense that she had difficulty finishing practices—even stand-ing could be painful—at age twelve. At fourteen, when she was swimming butterfly faster than any female in America, turning her neck sometimes made her arms go numb. When she finally climbed onto the starting blocks for the Olympic trials, Whitney was a surgeon's nightmare. In time, she was diagnosed with two bulging discs, a herniated disc, and two stress fractures.

For a long time, Whitney was angry about what hap-pened to her. Angry that she was permitted to swim through discomfort that turned to pain. Sad that what she views as benign neglect of her condition ultimately forced her out of the pool, making her abandon what was an all-consuming goal. She didn't want to talk about swimming. She avoided swim meets. At first, even sharing completely in her baby brother's successes was tough. Much time has passed. Whitney is married and a mother. She revels in Michael's successes, even assists in responding to his fan mail, which arrives by the truckload. In short, she's over it.

Yet she is frank discussing what her mother and her coach did and didn't do, how they viewed her swimming and what they may have sought from it. "My mom just wanted me to be the best. She saw the potential in me, the drive in me," she says. Yet even Debbie Phelps is not perfect. There were times when perhaps she might have seen a problem in the making. Whitney tells of a time she was at home in the Rodgers Forge neighborhood of Baltimore County with her mother and Michael. She had been training hard, and her back was not feeling all that great. "I bent down to get an apple out of the fridge. And I ... couldn't get back up. My mom or Michael came downstairs and found me sitting on the floor." It was a turning point, Whitney tells me. From then on her mother took very seriously each new report of pain in her back and legs. Before then, she says, "I was made to feel guilty about not practicing. My mom might say, 'Why don't you want to practice? Can't you go and do a little bit? Go and see what you can do.'" She doesn't blame her mom. "No one understood the extent of the injury."

Mention Murray Stephens to Whitney and suddenly the air is chilly.

"Murray just wanted a group of elite swimmers. There was a hardcore group of seven of us who swam together. We were workhorses. We would do whatever we had to do to be fast. Getting out of the pool [because you were hurt] might not have gone over so well. We were yelled at. And the way you were yelled at made you doubt yourself. You wondered: Is it that bad? Is it worth getting out or should I stick through for another five thousand yards?"

When I keep probing the subject with more "what ifs," Whitney finally interrupts. "That part of my life is over. But I definitely wonder what things would have been like if I could have stayed healthy and swam at the level that Michael has."

Debbie Phelps maintains that she mostly was in the dark about her daughter's injuries. She remembers being shocked after the disappointment at the Olympic trials to learn that Whitney's back troubles began at age ten. Her daughter had hidden that from her. "Never did it enter my mind," she says. She won't criticize Stephens; her family has had a long relationship with the stern but successful coach, and Michael Phelps remains in touch and on good terms with him. After Beijing, Michael and coach Bob Bowman returned to Meadowbrook in Baltimore and made it their home base again.

But Debbie speaks like a mother who took careful notes when Whitney's swim days ended, and she has applied those hard-earned lessons to overseeing her son's well-being in swimming. When I asked about Whitney, Debbie answered by quoting her daughter: "To this day, she says she wonders how good she could have been if she'd had Bob Bowman in her life."

Stephens couldn't have been thrilled to hear from me, a reporter wanting to talk about a swimmer named Phelps whose swim story ended unhappily. To his credit, he invited me to Meadowbrook and didn't duck any of my questions, though I had the feeling he wasn't all that impressed. It was a "simplification" to say Whitney's back hurt when she was ten, he told me, and not fair to his vaunted swim program to suggest that the North Baltimore Aquatic Club had pushed Whitney too hard. Olympic training is a demanding business, he explained. All involved take on certain risks. "There is no way you, the coach, the athlete, or even medical science is ever going to perfectly keep someone who is challenging their physical capabilities from possibly incurring a career-threatening injury."

During our two-hour meeting, Stephens explains that

training methods have changed since Whitney's day—swimmers log less pool time. Attitudes toward injury prevention also have evolved. "We have a couple guys with back issues right now. We try to work with it and try not to let it become chronic." As I am leaving, the coach extends an invitation to come back to the club to observe a practice. It will help me see the big picture, he says, and not get bogged down in the negative. "The media, they are looking for justification of their theme of the day, which is that adults drive children to injury and sickness because of their personal goals. I guess I am all about the positive. I know people will write these things, so I don't worry about it."

Rachel didn't want her real name used for reasons that, as she told me about her nightmare, I understood completely. She grew up in a large family in south Florida; of all her brothers and sisters, she had been the best athlete. She had talent and especially loved softball, which she began playing when she was in the third grade. Her father, a lawyer, took a close interest in her sports life. From the moment she started playing, he was her tutor, coach, and, she explained, tormentor. Softball practices were like boot camp, she told me. Mistakes were not acceptable. When she was nine years old, the penalty for an errant throw was to run around the school where the team worked out. "There were entire practices when all I did was cry," she recalls. The older she got, the more intense her father's behavior became. And scary. As he left the field one day, her brooding father swung a metal bat at a wooden post "with every bit of force in his body." Turning to his daughter, he said, "That's what I feel like doing right now *to you.*"

The drumbeat of criticism drained whatever fun was left in the sport for Rachel. When she'd started playing, she had dreamed of becoming a softball player in the Olympics. But before her senior year in high school, she decided to quit the sport. Breaking the news to her father was one of the hardest things she'd ever done. He was furious. For the next five months he shunned her, refusing to speak to her about her decision or anything else. "He told me I was making the biggest mistake of my life. He'd spent all that time and money so I could amount to a professional softball player, at least play in college, and get a free ride to some great school. He meant it was the biggest mistake of *his* life," she says. That was about five years ago. Rachel and her father still aren't close, but an emotional talk initiated by Rachel has begun the healing. She says he was startled to learn how his behavior had left such scars. "He felt terrible. He wanted us to go to group therapy."

As is the case with most revolutions, this one came with its share of unintended consequences, none more startling than the gold rush that has grown up around training a girl to be a college athlete. Just ask Michael McLaughlin. A dozen years ago, the Maryland divorce lawyer dreamt up the Sky Walkers Lacrosse Program. Now it's one of the best-known girls lacrosse clubs in the country, a veritable assembly line whose finished products are flashy college lacrosse players who stand out on many Division I teams. The University of North Carolina has suited up fifteen former Sky Walkers since 2001. Twenty-two have played college lacrosse in the Ivy League. All told, the club lists forty-nine different schools where McLaughlin has planted the Sky Walkers flag.

At any given time, there are about three hundred Sky Walkers, ranging from sixth graders to high school seniors. They practice for months at a time, go to out-of-town tournaments, and do basically whatever else McLaughlin and his staff of coaches direct them to. Some of it can be downright awful. One of McLaughlin's favorite conditioning drills is running young Sky Walkers up and down flights of stairs at full speed until they are physically spent or feeling so ill that they throw up. This happens so often that McLaughlin has a standard response to a child who staggers off the steps with an unsettled stomach: "If you're going to throw up, throw up. But when you're finished, get up and get back in."

The stern approach is necessary for children to get in touch with their inner lacrosse warrior or, as McLaughlin puts it, to master the sport's "mental aspect." Same for the repertoire of insults that McLaughlin has been known to hurl during particularly intense practices and games. McLaughlin readily acknowledges such behavior and, on request, even offers one of his favorite rants. "Here's one," he says without hesitating: "'My mother's dead and she can run faster than you!' [which I say] in the loudest voice I can, to make sure not only [the player] hears it but her teammates hear it and her parents hear it." Several parents described these tirades for me in minute detail, recalling McLaughlin's red face and loutish tone. One parent told me that his daughter had been on an opposing team playing the Sky Walkers when she witnessed one of McLaughlin's signature eruptions for the first time. The players found the coach's histrionics more than a little off-putting. The parent recalls his daughter "making a mental note that she'd never play for that guy." As her interest grew in playing lacrosse in college, though, she began to rethink that first impression. Several friends playing for the Sky Walkers convinced her that the club had boosted their games and, as significant, that it was possible to tune out the coach's yelling. Eventually, she accepted an invitation to join the club and, like a true Sky Walker, ended up playing lacrosse at a Division I school.

McLaughlin's unfiltered style can intimidate parents, too. One spoke with me at length about issues that he and his daughter had with the coach. Several weeks later, he called requesting that I forget about the interview. He hadn't been especially critical of McLaughlin, but the possibility that the coach would react badly to his comments had been weighing on him. A majority of parents spoke fondly of McLaughlin and their time with Sky Walkers. "What we were told before joining Sky Walkers was true: Mike McLaughlin is a maniac but a maniac with a heart of gold," says Scott Shane, a *New York Times* reporter whose daughter, Laura, went on from the club to become an All-American goalkeeper at Stanford.

Scott admitted that he and his wife, Francie, were "completely oblivious" to the recruiting rituals of college sports. "It's a miracle Laura ended up playing college sports because we were so out of it," he says.

Shane credits Sky Walkers, which his daughter joined her junior year in high school, for getting her much-needed exposure to college coaches. "She would not have been noticed by college coaches if she had not done that," Shane says. McLaughlin readily acknowledges that Sky Walkers isn't for everyone. "I tell the kids I can't fathom them going through this [training] if they don't have a goal of playing lacrosse in college. There are much easier things to do," he says. Then he sits back and reflects on what he views as the real value of the program. It sounds like a lesson in female empowerment. "I am an attorney. About fifty percent of the litigation I handle is in divorce courts. I see the tragedies of women who get married and are in the process of raising a family when a separation occurs and they have nothing," he says. "My real desire is to teach these kids that if they use this opportunity correctly they will never be dependent on a man. I never want a girl to work for a company when she can own the company."

Powerful sentiments, yet they can be overshadowed by the more immediate goal of securing a place to play college lacrosse. Virtually every girl in the club expects to be courted by college scouts, and many families are disappointed with anything less than a scholarship to play at a Division I school. If anything, McLaughlin heightens such expectations. When sixth graders enter the program, he tells their parents that college lacrosse will be the last stop. And through their years with Sky Walkers, McLaughlin keeps the heat on, pestering players to keep their grades up. There's no quarreling with the results. Yet there's something disquieting about a youth sports program in which every move is choreographed to advance the goal of a girl playing lacrosse in college. It seems to ignore a goal more important, even for girls so resilient they can withstand McLaughlin's guff for six long years. What about playing youth sports for sheer fun?

Tim Holley wonders what happened to that antiquated notion. The athletic director at the prestigious Gilman School in Baltimore is troubled that successful club programs like Sky Walkers perpetuate the false idea that a child's youth sports experience has a happy ending only if she winds up playing four years on the college varsity team. "That's absolutely wrong," says Holley, a former two-sport Ivy League athlete.

Holley speaks from experience. His daughter, a former high school lacrosse player, stuck with the sport until a dispiriting incident her sophomore year. She was playing for her school team, one of the best in the area, at a local lacrosse tournament. A number of college coaches attended, evaluating the better players and making introductions to those they planned to recruit. At the end of the day, Holley caught up with his daughter who, to his surprise, was in tears.

"What's wrong?" he asked, comforting her.

"Not a single coach wanted to speak with me. I guess I'm not going to college."

"Are you are playing because you want to go to college? If that's the case, quit right now," Holley recalls telling his daughter. "Play for fun."

"It's absolutely wrong," he says of the mindset. "When goals come before everything else, that's when sports become work. These kids are too young for that."

5   UNTIL IT HURTS

Marianne doesn't want her last name printed in this book. She also requested that her hometown be omitted, as well as anything else that even by the slimmest chance might reveal her identity or, far more important, her daughter's. The story she is about to tell isn't a happy one, and one not talked about openly in her home, even six years later. She's agreed to tell her story here as a cautionary tale.

Her daughter was eleven years old. She loved swimming, and she was terrific at it. Marianne was pleased and then amazed at her progress. She won a state open-water competition. Then she started catching up with older girls on her club team. One day, she came home from practice and excitedly shared her news with Marianne: The coach was moving her up. From now on she'd be training with a group of high school girls.

Marianne was proud, of course, but also uneasy that the coach had announced the decision to her daughter without her approval or even input. Other things happening at the pool concerned her too. She recalls being at a workout when the team's hard-charging coach summoned a dozen or so swimmers to the side of the pool. Unaware Marianne was

within earshot, the coach began berating the girls. He repeated over and over that because they'd swum so poorly
that afternoon they'd squandered the privilege of attending
a much-anticipated school function that weekend. "I don't
want to hear the H-word. I don't want to hear the H-word,"
the coach bellowed repeatedly. He was declaring the home-
coming dance off-limits.

Other things about the swim team seemed skewed. The
coach was measuring the swimmers' body fat, her daughter
told her. At practices, he'd bring out a pair of calipers and
move from girl to girl pinching arms. He was insisting on
drawing blood from the swimmers, too. Again, Marianne
hadn't granted permission and, in fact, was hearing about it
for the first time.

Did Marianne mention the schedule? In a word, it was
exhausting: practices seven days a week, including two hours
on Saturday mornings and three hours on Sunday afternoons. Off days? Almost too few to mention. The team got
a week off in April, a week in August, then Thanksgiving,
Christmas, and Easter. "It was like being in a war zone. Go
to the pool. Leave the pool. That's all you do," she says.

In that pressure cooker, very little seemed beyond the
pale, including the improbable story that Marianne's daughter carried home in 2002. The coach had scheduled a marathon swim. Marianne had never heard the term. On New
Year's Eve, the team would stage an all-nighter, swimming
up and down the pool in three-hour shifts until they'd
logged twenty-four hours and twenty-seven miles, almost
the circumference of Manhattan. The idea sounded crazy
to Marianne, but not much crazier than other things she'd
already permitted her daughter to take part in. Besides, her
child was thrilled. "This was heaven for her," Marianne says,
recalling that she gushed, "'Mom, twenty-four hours and all
we do is sleep and swim!'"

On marathon day, Marianne warily dropped off her
daughter at the pool and wished her luck. She returned the

next morning at nine. Her daughter was not in the pool. Marianne found her slumped on the pool deck, her elbow encased in ice. She was not smiling.

It was an overuse injury. After a few weeks off, her elbow improved. Then, after going back to practice, it ached again. The ups and downs were hard to take. Seeking an answer, Marianne took her daughter to orthopedic surgeons in three states. Still her elbow didn't respond. The coach made matters worse by poking fun at the injury and challenging the young swimmer's courage. The taunting gnawed at her, then made her sicker. She developed a gastrointestinal disorder from the anxiety. Before practice each day she'd reach into her backpack for a bowl and vomit.

For months, Marianne says, she agonized over whether to step in and yank her daughter away from swimming but decided for her daughter's sake she shouldn't. "She had to come to this decision on her own or she would have resented me forever."

The family's youth sports nightmare ended that year. Marianne's daughter, then thirteen, called from the pool to announce she had decided to stop swimming. Marianne recalls it as liberation day. She also remembers saying to her daughter, "I'm so proud of you."

Now, three years later, Marianne is willing to share the whole distressing story because she hopes telling it will put other parents on alert. Don't allow children to play sports until it hurts. "I saw my daughter suffer physical, mental, and emotional pain over swimming," she says. "And I think she still suffers."

Patrick Grady can relate. Even twenty-seven years after playing his last Little League game, he still can't forgive coaches and league officials for what they took from him.

At the time, Grady was twelve years old and playing Little League baseball in Westchester County, New York. By his account, he was one of the league's star pitchers, striking out most of the batters he faced and winning almost all the games he pitched. His coaches were impressed. They pitched him constantly. During his two Little League seasons, Grady estimates that he was his team's pitcher in two-thirds of its games. There are Little League rules to prevent such abuse. But as Grady recalls, his coaches disregarded them, and league officials didn't object.

Even when Grady's arm began to show alarming signs of overuse, grownups failed to step in. First his elbow ached. Then he began to lose feeling in his pinkie and ring fingers. Through it all he kept pitching. During an all-star game featuring the most talented players from the local league, Grady was the pitcher and alerted his coach to a terrible pain. When rain delayed the game for a while, the coach led Grady off the diamond to the snack bar. There, Grady insists, the coach stuck his star pitcher's arm in the freezer next to the ice pops, so that with his arm at thirty-degree temperature, "I'd be numb enough to pitch the last four innings."

Grady's coaches presumably got what they wanted from their Little League experiences. With the aid of their top-notch pitcher, they had the thrill of seeing their teams win championships. They lived out their dreams and showed off their coaching prowess for approving parents and other spectators. The cost to Patrick Grady was high. His dream of playing for a college or even a high school baseball team never materialized. At fifteen, he had surgery to transpose a nerve in his elbow and never pitched again. "My potential career in baseball vaporized," he says.

Make no mistake: Injuries are inherent to youth sports, as inevitable as car pools and grass stains. In 2003, more than 3.5 million children under age fifteen suffered a sports injury that required medical treatment—about one attended injury for every ten players. Many were the result of garden-variety mishaps: a base runner turning an ankle at second base or a field hockey goalie nicked by a point-blank shot.

Yet within the statistics is a hidden stat not as easily shrugged off. Each year, as many as half of all youth sports injuries are the result of overuse—a regimen of sports play and training so intense that a child's body rebels. In some high-volume clinics, the picture is still worse. Lyle Micheli, the youth sports medicine pioneer, estimates that of the seventy young patients who file into his clinic each Thursday at Children's Hospital Boston, 75 percent are victims of overuse injuries—soccer players with tender knees, swimmers whose shoulders hang like limp spaghetti, and the never-ending line of baseball pitchers accompanied by their aching elbows. Back in the early 1990s, the figure was at about 20 percent. That tells Micheli that in his decades-long battle against overuse injuries, the frayed muscle fibers and inflamed tendons are winning. "As a medical society, we've been pretty ineffective dealing with this," he says. "Nothing seems to be working."

What makes overuse injuries so infuriating to the Michelis of the world are two simple truths. First, unlike traumatic injuries—dislocations, hyperextensions, and other mishaps—injuries caused by overuse are easily prevented. By introducing variety, moderation, and rest into an everyday sports routine, a child's risk can be cut to nearly zero. Second, adults are the great enablers of overuse injuries. Where we go, ruptured ligaments and chronic tendonitis inevitably follow. Before the adult-dominated era of youth sports, "We didn't talk about these kinds of injuries, at least in the [medical] literature," notes Dr. John DiFiori, chief of sports medicine at UCLA's Comprehensive Sports Medicine Center and physician for UCLA's intercollegiate sports teams. And for good reason. Until parents showed up there wasn't much to discuss. Children entertaining themselves at their own pace, in their own way, simply did not play sports until it hurt. "Little League shoulder, tennis elbow, you don't see it unless kids are in an organized sport," notes DiFiori.

It's not just pitcher's elbow. And it's not just adolescent boys. The rainbow of overuse injuries is strikingly diverse. In an average year, pediatric sports medicine specialist Eric Small treats children who've overdone it in baseball, basketball, track, figuring skating, volleyball, and football. "I see one or two fencers a year," he says, and their issues are no joke—wrist and elbow tendonitis and sometimes a condition known as thoracic outlet syndrome, a pinched nerve in the shoulder blade that leaves its victims with numbness in their fingers and hands. Two-thirds of Small's patients are girls, many suffering the King Kong of girls sports injuries—ACL tears. The age of overuse patients also is cause for alarm— it's falling fast. Pediatrician Rebecca Demorest, who practices at New York City's Hospital for Special Surgery, sees youth baseball pitchers ushered into her waiting room at age eight.

The American Academy of Pediatrics is worried enough to have issued two policy statements on overuse injuries in three years, the latest in 2007. Says pediatrician Joel Brenner, its principal author, "We always hear about the obesity epidemic. Yet, on the other end of the spectrum, there's definitely a group of kids who are too active."

For every overuse injury, there's a story of a risk recognized too late or an adult's burning ambition left unchecked. Orthopedic surgeon Scott Maughon recalls an anxious mother who came to his Atlanta office with her ten-year-old daughter, a tennis player with an aching shoulder. The mother explained to Maughon that her daughter was rapidly climbing the Georgia state junior tennis rankings. To meet the family's goals for her, the girl had two weeks to reach number 5. Maughon tells me that, during an exam, he diagnosed a stress fracture, a potentially serious injury that could interfere with the normal growth of the girl's shoulder. He explained to the mother that her daughter should take an extended break from tennis of up to six months. It wasn't the answer the mother had come for. As Maughon recalls, she flew into a "yelling, screaming, stomping" rage, assailing the doctor for being overly cautious and insisting that her daughter didn't need any time off—she could be treated just as well with physical therapy. "It was one of those cases where a parent absolutely, totally refuses to deal with reality," says Maughon. "Do parents think I get a thrill out of shutting a kid down? That I'm telling them their child needs rest when their child doesn't need rest? You can go to a chiropractor. Wish on a star. Try a magnet. Wear garlic. The fact of the matter is your child needs rest."

DiFiori recalls a mother bringing her ten-year-old son to his office with complaints of a pain in his knee. The boy was a gifted soccer player, and his father was his coach. DiFiori diagnosed the boy with a growth-plate injury, similar to ones suffered by gymnasts and marathon runners. Growth plates are areas of growing tissue at the ends of bones in children. They're among the weakest structures in the human skeleton—weaker than ligaments and tendons, which join bones to one another. Growth-plate injuries among youth athletes are common—and often serious. A damaged growth plate may interfere with the normal growth of a child's bone.

The injury clearly was the result of overuse. From the mother, DiFiori learned that the boy had been playing soccer nearly nonstop, multiple games and practices each week, for two years. The previous year, he had just two weeks off. DiFiori prescribed a lengthy break. The mother approved and, within a year, the boy had recovered. In the life of a sports medicine physician, the case was uneventful stuff. DiFiori recalls it vividly only because of the reaction of the boy's father to the diagnosis—angry and defiant. "He kept asking, 'How could he have this injury? Why does he have to stop playing?' Later, I got an e-mail from the mother thanking me and apologizing for [her husband's] behavior."

The father's reluctance to accept his son's diagnosis troubled DiFiori. "You have a kid who is not capable intellectually of understanding the situation and a parent who is insisting on behavior resulting in an injury," DiFiori says. "Some people would have viewed it as child abuse."

Joseph Chandler has had similar issues with adults he had not even met yet. When he was the team doctor for the Atlanta Braves, the parents of youth pitchers in the area often would seek him out in times of great urgency. Unlike other patients who explained their problems when they came to the office, these moms and dads would call weeks before their appointments, Chandler remembers, with warnings like, "'I can't really talk about this in front of my son. But you need to understand that he has big league potential; he's something special!'" Chandler says, "It floored me. What kind of pressure must twelve-year-old kids be under from their parents?"

It's not *all* our fault. There is no shortage of cultural cues to disable a parent's normally good sense. The pressure to compete, to win, to stay even with the family next door recedes at times, but it is the rare family that banishes it altogether. Sports psychologist Richard Ginsburg likens it to a river's current that, once waded into, requires great effort to escape. "Once the flow grabs you and takes you, it's hard to step back," he says.

Then there is the coterie of adult accomplices who stand ready to help a child get to the next level—professional coaches. In individual sports such as gymnastics, figure skating, and tennis, they're ubiquitous. Every child needs one, and just about every child has one. Such coaches can spend several hours with a young athlete each day, honing skills and, in healthy relationships, building friendship and trust. But when the ambition of the child, the coach, or both, goes unchecked, things can go terribly wrong.

In her book *Little Girls in Pretty Boxes,* author Joan Ryan tells stories almost too bizarre to believe about training that apparently was routine in the world of elite figure skating and gymnastics. Ryan writes about fourteen-year-old Kristie Phillips, destined to be the next Mary Lou Retton, training with a broken wrist while gulping twelve Advil and six prescription anti-inflammatories each day. Then there's Betty Okino, then seventeen, competing for the U.S. women's gymnastics team in the 1992 Olympics with stress fractures in her back and elbow—and a tendon in her shin held in place with a screw.

Eric Small has treated patients whom he feared would be

similarly damaged by their sports. He recalls a figure skater, just eleven years old, who came to his office complaining of pain in her leg. Small diagnosed the problem as a muscle strain and tendonitis. Yet the problem did not go away, and the girl kept returning to his office over the next few months. Concerned, Small probed her about her training regimen and learned the child was being passed around by eight skating coaches. *Eight!* In his long experience dealing with overtrained kids, he'd never heard of anything like it. "One for choreography, one for jumping, one for movement, and I don't know what the other five did," he says, still amazed. Small explained to the girl's parents that, even if all the coaches stayed, their daughter's jump training had to be dialed back.

Some children beset by sports injuries do it all, or mostly all, on their own. Samantha Slonim injured her knee playing softball and had her first ACL reconstruction at age thirteen. At the time, her sports year consisted of travel softball, travel soccer, school volleyball, and school basketball. "I forget which seasons overlapped," Samantha says now. Later she had two more operations on the same knee—an arthroscopic repair and a second ACL reconstruction. Weary of rehab, she gave up competitive sports her junior year of high school. She's philosophical and somewhat nostalgic about her former sports life. "I was just sort of fearless. I got hurt all the time," she says. Now a student at DePaul University College of Law, her injuries still speak to her. During the bitter cold Chicago winters, the screws buried deep in her knee act up. Even now, she says, "I can't really run on it."

Christy Hammond would settle for being able to get around normally. Her youth sports ordeal has left her unable to walk or even stand for long without pounding in her left knee. She can't recall a pain-free day for nearly five years. "My parents never pushed me," she says. "But being active and playing sports all my life, I would not let myself quit until it was too late. Today, I would kill just to be able to walk and stand without chronic and intense knee pain."

Christy's story isn't that different from other sports-centered girls, which makes it all the more frightening.

She grew up a tomboy, preferring to play sports with boys and never wanting to stop. By the sixth grade, she'd tried her hand at swimming, gymnastics, ballet, soccer, volleyball, soccer, track, basketball, and even the untomboy-like sport of cheerleading. Her body started protesting early. At thirteen, Christy was playing soccer and tore her ACL. Two years later, during a high school basketball tryout, the ACL ruptured completely. The idea that she might give up competitive sports never seriously entered her mind, Christy says. Six months after ACL surgery, she was back running laps with her high school track team. Her parents urged her to slow down but she wouldn't—couldn't—listen. "In gym class, I'd play basketball even though I knew they were against it. When they found out they'd scream and yell, 'Christy, your knee is bad enough.' I'm a stubborn person. I didn't want to be sitting on the sidelines."

By her sophomore year, Hammond's pain had returned and her knee had to be repaired twice more. Since then, there have been more surgeries and, she offers, in no particular order, ten MRIs, four bone scans, several cortisone shots, a lidocaine infusion, acupuncture treatments, hypnosis, psychotherapy—and no relief. To dull the throb in her knee, she takes Vicodin nearly every day.

Now a sports marketing and communication studies major at the University of Michigan and a sports blogger at Behindthejersey.com, Hammond faces a life in some ways more restricted than her friends'. She can't bike, swim, or work out at the gym, as they do. After a Wolverines football game, the highlight of a fall week on campus, she detours around the tailgate parties and heads back to her dorm. After a few hours on her damaged knee, "I can't do anything the rest of the evening."

ACLs are a conundrum all to themselves. The acronym is shorthand for anterior cruciate ligament, one of the four sinewy strands that run beneath the kneecap, connecting the thigh bone with the shin bone. ACLs are knee stabilizers that work hardest when athletes jump, twist, or cut to the goal. And on athletic fields where girls are playing sports, they're under siege.

Seen in real time, an ACL rupture isn't easily forgotten. There's an unmistakable popping sound usually followed by a horrific scream. Each year, one out of a hundred high school female athletes and a stunning 10 percent of college female athletes suffer an ACL injury. Female athletes have a four to eight times higher incidence of the knee injury than men. Patients generally require reconstruction surgery at a cost of about $25,000. Next comes six to eight months of intense rehabilitation and, for a majority of patients, a return to sports.

Bruce Reider, a nationally known orthopedic surgeon in Chicago, notes that when he started in practice, "We didn't see nearly the number of female patients we see now." That was nearly thirty years ago, not long after the passage of Title IX and cultural enlightenment about gender equity in sports. Then Reider makes a fascinating observation about sports injuries and girls during that period. "There was an almost condescending attitude among physicians. If a girl had an injury, it wasn't worrisome because she could always stop participating. As opposed to boys who, of course, had to get back to sports participation," he says. "Obviously, the social context has changed since then. I have seen my own attitudes change, too."

ACL injuries are now so common that they have been known to wipe out not only star players, but starting lineups, as Castle High School in Evansville, Indiana, can attest. In 2005, the Castle High girls basketball team lost three-fifths of its lineup during a sixteen-day ACL siege. "It's just amazing" was all that Castle coach Wayne Allen could say to the *Evansville Courier* at the time. ACL injuries run in families, too. Twin sisters Trista and Kaela Munster played basketball and soccer together and were freshmen stars of the 1,600-meter relay team at Grant Community High School near Chicago.

Before their sophomore years, both had ruptured ACLs. "Well, I did it. Now you have to do it," Trista told Kaela after her injury, notes the *Chicago Daily Herald*.

Whether ACL injuries are truly caused by overuse is its own debate, though mostly one for surgeons and other sports doctors. Letha Y. Griffin, an orthopedic surgeon in Atlanta who has long experience repairing ACLs in girls, doesn't see a link to overuse. She maintains girls are vulnerable for a few reasons. The anatomy of young girls predisposes them to the injury. Typically, a girl's pelvis is wider than a boy's, making her thigh bones angle down more sharply. The greater that angle, the more pressure is exerted on the knee during sports play and the higher the risk of ACL tears. Faulty conditioning is another variable. Weak hamstrings and strong quadriceps are the downfall of thousands of ACL patients each year. Then there's just plain exhaustion. Tired athletes are running, cutting, and pivoting on tired knees. And, Griffin says, "Fatigued muscles don't respond as quickly" as rested ones.

From his office in Mount Kisco, Eric Small agrees wholeheartedly with the last point. As evidence, he offers a profile of his ACL patients. Most are stars who play nearly every minute of every game. And significantly, he believes, many suffer their injuries on national holidays—Memorial Day for field hockey and lacrosse players, Labor Day for soccer players. The patients aren't leaving the field to attend family barbecues. Typically, they'd been playing in all-day tournaments in which one team might be on the field for five or six games. After hour upon hour of bobbing and weaving, "muscles fatigue and an injury is more likely," Small notes. His broad definition of overuse injuries encompasses such cases.

Joe Chandler is a trim, mustachioed man with a piercing voice that squeaks higher when he laughs, which is often. A first meeting with him ends with Chandler shaking hands and opening his arms to give a visitor a bear hug. He spent the first half of his professional life in the operating room inserting screws and pins into broken bones. He ran a busy orthopedic practice in Atlanta and was team orthopedist for the Braves, caring for the million-dollar arms of star pitchers such as Tom Glavine and John Smoltz. Over the last half of his career, he hopes to do as much for eight- and nine-year-old baseball pitchers.

Chandler's changed course was not entirely voluntary. In 1997, while performing surgery, he damaged his hand, an injury that eventually forced him out of the operating room. He continued seeing patients, however, including many with overuse baseball injuries. At that same time, overuse injuries were spiking among pitchers in the Braves minor league organization. Chandler wondered why. He knew the Braves weren't responsible—he had the pitch logs proving that. But what was? Curious, he quizzed Braves players, trying to piece together their baseball lives as children. How old had they been when they became pitchers? When had they thrown their first curveball?

Then, Chandler embarked on another project. For years he'd watched the Little League World Series on TV, marveling at the poise and talent of the young pitchers. The laws of probability, if nothing else, dictated that some would become stars in professional baseball. Yet, as far as Chandler knew, none had. Somewhere between the little green diamonds in Williamsport and the 50,000-seat ballpark where Chandler worked in Atlanta, these young pitchers were vanishing. It didn't fit with Little League Baseball's record of keeping youth players safe, one that officials deservedly call attention to and take pride in. After all, it was Little League Baseball that introduced batting helmets with ear flaps in 1959. And Little League Baseball has stayed on message under Stephen Keener, the organization's president and CEO since 1994, banning on-deck circles (to protect waiting batters from being slammed by batted balls) and, beginning in 2008, mandating breakaway bases, to reduce injuries from tumbling awkwardly into the next base.

Those safety steps are progressive and, for the most part,

uncontroversial. They keep players in the game—end of story. Pitching rules are a far more complicated proposition because they balance interests at the heart of Little League Baseball. On the one hand, young pitching arms must not be overworked. On the other, every coach wants his ace on the mound for the big game.

For fifty years, the only protection offered to youth pitchers was a rule limiting them to six innings in a week of games. The rule was easily enforced, but skirted the issue of greatest concern—the number of pitches children toss during those innings. Chandler decided to count. He acquired videos of old Little League World Series, and with assistance from Braves minor league players, he noted each pitch. In 2006, Chandler and Nick Crocker, a former Braves minor-league player, repeated the exercise, this time screening all thirty-two world series games and an eye-bugging 3,798 pitches.

The data was startling. Some Little Leaguers in Williamsport, Chandler and Crocker discovered, worked as hard as grown men pitching in big league ballparks. In the clinching game of the 2007 World Series, Red Sox starting (and winning) pitcher Jon Lester tossed 92 pitches—one less pitch than those thrown on average by kids who tossed complete games in the 2006 Little League World Series (a complete game in Little League is six innings). One overworked lad threw a Nolan Ryan–esque 116 pitches.

Data on curveballs was just as surprising. Curveballs are hard to hit pitches designed to dart over and around the bats of opposing hitters. They're thrown differently than other pitches, often with a wrist snap and twist of the elbow that puts added stress on developing arms. Anyone who has watched a Little League World Series knows that curveballs are as much a part of the scene at Williamsport as cotton candy and souvenir programs. Chandler's research showed just how curve-happy the annual tournament had become. In the 2001 championship game, for instance, the surgeon's analysis showed pitchers for teams from Tokyo and Apopka, Florida, tossing curves an astonishing 64 percent of the time.

Chandler wasn't alone in trying to rouse Little League Baseball. James Andrews also was making a racket. Andrews is the James Brown of orthopedic surgery—the hardest-working man in the operating room and a prolific researcher, too. With Glenn Fleisig, his colleague at the renowned American Sports Medicine Institute, the research arm of Andrews's surgical center in Birmingham, Alabama, Andrews has devoted years to the study of overuse injuries, probing the risks to the human arm when it whips thousands of pitches over hundreds of games. Their studies are arcane to some, endlessly fascinating to others. (One finding: Pitchers who throw more than eighty pitches in a game have four times the risk of injury leading to surgery compared to pitchers who don't.) There's no doubt that they have painted a remarkable and alarming picture of how easy it is to destroy a young player's future.

Little League Baseball listens to Andrews and Fleisig—to a point. In 2004, when the duo joined USA Baseball, a governing body for the sport, in offering safety recommendations for kid pitchers, the powers that be in Williamsport got the message. For the first time Keener and the Little League front office embraced mandatory pitch counts. But rather than accept limits proposed by Andrews and Fleisig—seventy-five pitches per game and a maximum of one hundred pitches in a week—Little League arrived at its own watered-down standards: eighty-five pitches in a game and allowing eleven-year-olds to throw those eighty-five pitches after three days of rest. That doesn't include warm-up pitches before the game and the ten or so tosses from the mound between innings. The new rules place no restrictions on those.

The situation is more troubling during the Little League postseason—the world series and the qualifying tournaments leading up to that famous event. In those games, young pitchers can go to the mound on two days' rest, creating the unhappy possibility of a child throwing an arm-numbing 255 pitches in a week. That has almost happened. In the 2007 tournament, according to the *Sports Business Journal,* pitchers from teams in Minnesota, Oregon, and Texas all threw 230 to 240 pitches in one week. Kyle Cotcamp of Ohio tossed an incredible 267 in nine days. If the New York Yankees asked any of their grownup pitchers to do the same, they'd have a revolt on their hands.

Little League Baseball's decades-old tolerance of curveballs is just as puzzling. In August 2005, I wrote an article for the *New York Times* under the headline "Warnings for Children Are Clear, but Curveballs Are Rising, Not Sinking." The piece explained that curveballs had become an accepted part of Little League Baseball, a curiosity given that everyone from doctors to professional baseball players believed they should be outlawed for kid pitchers. Joe Chandler was quoted saying he believed strongly that children should not begin to throw curveballs until they were at least fourteen. Professional pitchers surveyed by Chandler were even more cautious, saying they wouldn't allow their sons to learn the pitch until they'd nearly turned fifteen. Even Little League's Keener came across as anticurve in the article, saying, "We are hearing from more and more medical professionals that the danger is there." Curves are getting closer scrutiny these days. In 2006, Little League Baseball joined a five-year study led by researchers at the University of North Carolina looking into the effects of the pitches on the arms of youngsters. By my count, that would make the results available after 2010, Little League Baseball's seventy-second anniversary. The adults don't seem to be in a great hurry.

As usual, my hands were not clean. I refused to teach my son to throw a curveball during the formative years when I was his coach—from age seven stretching beyond his thirteenth birthday. I knew better. I had witnessed other children blow out their arms that way. Still, I wanted my son to have an edge. That was always my problem. And, by extension, Ben's. At twelve, he was a good pitcher with the tools to become an even better one. I really did not need to rush him or interfere with his progress. But of course I did. I taught him a pitch I had thrown in high school, when I was sixteen. It wasn't a curveball per se, so I could tell myself that there was no danger to his arm. But looking back, it wasn't a pitch I'd want another dad sharing with my son. Not only did Ben throw it, he wrote about it. That summer, he spent a week at Little League's sleepover summer baseball camp. When he returned home, Ben landed an assignment to write a kid's account of life at such camps, based on his considerable experience as a consumer of summer baseball instruction (and marshmallow roasts). About four months later, readers of *USA Today*'s *Baseball Weekly* were hearing about young Ben's adventures in Williamsport, including his estimable efforts to confuse fellow campers with a trick pitch "my father taught me." I'd been exposed. Humbled, too. Yet true to form, the first thing I wanted to know was whether he threw it for a strike.

6   MIRACLES FOR ALL

Any examination of kids' sports and overuse injuries would be sorely lacking if it did not pay homage to Frank Jobe, as close to an icon as exists in the field of sports medicine. Jobe is a member of one hall of fame—the American Orthopaedic Society for Sports Medicine—and a legion of his grateful ex-patients believe time is long overdue for his induction into another—the National Baseball Hall of Fame. "They ought to build a medical wing," Orel Hershiser, a former great Los Angeles Dodger whose pitching career was saved by the surgeon, has said. In his modest office at the Kerlan-Jobe Orthopaedic Clinic, outside Los Angeles, the walls are lined with photographs of a sampling of the hundreds of professional athletes patched up by Jobe over five decades. They range from the small (Triple Crown–winning jockey Willie Shoemaker) to the tall (basketball giant Wilt Chamberlain), from an international hero (Japanese home-run king Sadaharu Oh) to an American hero (the incomparable Los Angeles Dodgers pitcher Sandy Koufax), and to a patient who may be the most remarkable success story of Jobe's long career. His name is Tommy John.

It's fitting that when Jobe steps into his office, one of the first faces he sees is John's, smiling down from a picture frame next to a long window. Nearly four decades ago, the resourceful surgeon and the stubborn ballplayer made medical history together. John's contribution was destroying the ligament in his left elbow on the pitcher's mound at Dodger Stadium. Jobe's was recognizing that he might be able to reconstruct it. The surgeon succeeded beyond anyone's wildest dreams, including his own. The operation he conceived allowed John to extend his career an amazing fourteen years. Its significance was far greater than one man's elbow, though. Jobe's genius changed an entire sport. Suddenly, pitching arms had a second life, and sometimes a third. (One unfortunate soul, former big league pitcher José Rijo, supposedly had Tommy John surgery five times.) The operation might have come along eventually without Jobe, but who can tell? At the very least he was years ahead of his time. Dr. Lewis Yocum, who trained under Jobe and now works with him at the Kerlan-Jobe Orthopaedic Clinic, believes Jobe might just know more about baseball and pitching injuries than anyone.

The furthest thing from Jobe's mind when he dreamed up the surgery was that someday the patients undergoing it would be teenagers. His intention was to save the career of a grown man, one who happened to be among the finest pitchers in Major League Baseball. By the 1990s, Tommy John surgery had proved stunningly reliable in repairing the arms of major league pitchers. The operation's success rate—defined as pitchers able to return to the level at which they performed before their injuries—topped 80 percent. Major league pitchers no longer feared the surgery and, in fact, began viewing it as a nip-and-tuck procedure they'd need eventually if they pitched long enough. One in seven current pitchers in the big leagues has had the career-saving surgery. No doubt, most have scant knowledge of the man behind it.

Frank W. Jobe did not start life as the patron saint of elbows. He grew up far from operating rooms and professional baseball players in Greensboro, North Carolina. Jobe might have lived his whole life in Greensboro if not for World War

II. At eighteen, he joined the war effort as a medic in the Army's 101st Airborne Division. On the front lines in Europe, he tended to Yank troops and narrowly avoiding capture at the Battle of the Bulge, where nineteen thousand Americans died. During the war, Jobe spent so much time with doctors he began to think seriously about becoming one. When he returned home in 1946, he moved to California and attended college on the GI Bill, then borrowed what he needed to put himself through Loma Linda Medical School. For a while, he was a family practice doctor, tending to strep throats and occasionally delivering babies. After treating several patients with broken bones, he got the idea to study orthopedics. He was accepted into a residency program at the University of Southern California and, while there, met a witty, wise-cracking surgeon named Robert Kerlan. For the next thirty years, the duo formed the most successful and durable partnership in sports medicine, caring for Chamberlain, Shoemaker, and hundreds of other world-famous patients.

These days, the Kerlan-Jobe Orthopaedic Clinic is a sports medicine kingdom, with twenty-one surgeons, three offices, and a biomechanics laboratory, where sports injuries in children are studied each day. Kerlan died in 1996, but Jobe, well past his eightieth birthday, still comes to his office most days and has no plans to stop. "As long as my brain works, I don't think I'll retire as such," he says. He still assists in the operating room, still is the top medicine man of the Dodgers and the PGA Tour, and every Thursday sees patients who want answers just as Tommy John did in 1974.

The night of July 17, 1974, was warm and typically pleasant in Los Angeles; Frank Jobe was in his club-level seats behind home plate. A large crowd gathered at Dodger Stadium to watch the best pitcher in baseball. Tommy John, thirty-one years old, breezed through the first two innings before getting into trouble in the third. Montreal Expos base runners were at first and second base. At bat stood Hal Breeden, a journeyman ballplayer who could tighten the game with one swing. Peering in at the plate, John's only thought was to throw a ball low in the strike zone, one that Breeden would pound into the grass for an easy double play. Nobody could have guessed that his next pitch would be his last in a big league game for nearly two years.

John looked in for the sign and rocked back. As his left arm whipped forward, he felt "the strangest sensation I had ever known. A nothing sensation, as if the arm wasn't there."

The pitch did not cross home plate, though its exact whereabouts after leaving John's left hand are in dispute these days. John writes in his autobiography, "The ball just blooped up to the plate and the catcher took it well out of the strike zone." Jobe, who attended most Dodger games, recalls something more dramatic: the baseball arcing high over the catcher's head and dropping into the stands, where it scattered fans in the first few rows. "It was a bad pitch, I know that much," Jobe says, laughing.

As soon as he reached John in the Dodger clubhouse, Jobe knew the pitcher was injured horribly. Taking John's elbow in his hands, Jobe applied pressure to the joint; it swung open like a broken hinge. Almost certainly, that meant the ulnar collateral ligament (UCL) was badly damaged and perhaps torn straight through. Either way, John was finished as a baseball player. No one with the injury had ever recovered to pitch again, as far as Jobe knew. "We'd say they 'blew their arm out' and that was the end of it."

John was not other pitchers. He was stubborn and pushy. When Jobe broke the news that his career might not be salvageable, he refused to accept the doctor's pragmatic view. Jobe recalls John telling him that he was willing to try the most radical, experimental treatments; the bottom line was that he had to pitch again and Jobe had to help.

Jobe began to plan. To save John's career, he had to stabilize the pitcher's elbow with something strong yet pliable. In short, something like the ligament that John had destroyed. Perhaps a tendon might do it. Jobe knew of operations in which tendons were transplanted to repair hands. Polio patients also had transplants to bolster weak joints. Jobe had done a few of those operations himself, though nothing like what John might need. Still, the experience focused his thinking. Jobe began contemplating how to adapt the surgery, even sketching out a tendon transplant operation. It was no sure bet. Even if he succeeded, Jobe had no idea whether the graft would stand up to the stress of a grown man hurling a baseball.

On September 25, Jobe operated on John at Centinela Valley Hospital in Inglewood. Save for the patient and the surgeon, the significance of the event was lost on everyone. The *Los Angeles Times* reported on the operation on page 6 of the sports section: "A tendon from pitcher Tommy John's right forearm was used in the reconstruction of his left elbow during a two-hour operation...Team physician Frank Jobe, who performed the surgery, said he is 'optimistic' about the outcome but he added, 'we won't be able to tell a great deal until spring training.'" The *New York Times* paid less attention, noting John's operation on page 30, sandwiched between a news item about NBA rookie Bill Walton's hyperextended elbow and Billie Jean King being named most valuable player of World Team Tennis.

Jobe was unsure when John would be well enough to pitch again. He wasn't sure about setbacks either. John had one a few weeks after the surgery. Scar tissue built up near the tendon graft, binding up the ulnar nerve. The pitcher's fingers receded into a claw. In December, Jobe had to operate again.

The 1975 baseball season was lost to John. He spent his days squeezing balls of putty, soaking his hand in the whirlpool bath, and largely being the object of pity. Many of his Dodger teammates thought he was wasting his time. It took John one more year to prove they were wrong. On April 28, 1976, the Dodgers played the Pittsburgh Pirates. For the first time in nearly two years, the winning pitcher in a major league baseball game was Tommy John. It wasn't the last.

Before his surgery, John had never won twenty games in a season. After his surgery, he won twenty games in a season three times. All told, 164 of John's 288 career-pitching victories came after Frank Jobe's miracle.

Today, the operation invented to save John's career is available to almost anyone. Frank Jobe's son Christopher, also an orthopedic surgeon, operated on California congressman Joe Baca, who ruptured his ulnar collateral ligament while practicing for a pick-up baseball game among members of Congress. And of course there is the alarming number of youth patients. Not that long ago, it was rare for a surgeon to operate on an athlete not yet of college age. From 1988 to 1994, renowned Alabama-based surgeon James Andrews performed Tommy John surgery on just seven high school players. From 2000 to 2004, that figure climbed to 124. Today more than half of the Tommy John operations that Andrews does are on high school and college athletes. Tim Kremchek, an orthopedic surgeon in Cincinnati, says he has performed the operation on patients as young as nine or ten.

Is Tommy John surgery a little too miraculous? Too available? These are odd questions to ask about an operation that has helped thousands of athletes, maybe tens of thousands. In a real sense, the answer appears to be yes. Thanks to the operation, repairing a child's elbow ligament has become nearly routine. Destroying the elbow of that child with too much pitching doesn't seem like a big deal either. The operation has given license to overzealous parents and coaches. If they were willing to take a chance before, there's less stopping them now. Lewis Yocum performs as many Tommy John operations as almost any surgeon in the country and meets dozens of sore-armed teenagers each year. He told me that some of their parents not only are eager for their children to have the surgery, they actually view the operation as a credential that establishes a youth player as an athlete with a future worth protecting. "You hear them [parents] talking in the waiting room," he says. " 'My son is having Tommy John.

He's obviously big league material because he sustained the injury and now he has to have the operation.'"

Yocum and other top doctors question whether adults have lost sight of the operation's purpose. Rather than seeing it as a treatment of last resort, some have the impression that the surgery is a performance enhancer, one that can increase a child's pitching speed. (Not true, say doctors.) Others fail to realize that the operation they're seeking out, though much safer since John went under the knife, is still an operation and still carries risk.

An excellent article by Jere Longman in the *New York Times* makes this point. Longman reported on an athletic trainer in Nashville who'd polled high school and college baseball players with sound arms for their views on Tommy John surgery. When the trainer asked if the operation would boost their effectiveness, nine of forty-six responded yes. In the article, Longman also included an interview with a family in Tennessee that recently had been through a Tommy John surgery. The father of the patient, a sixteen-year-old high school pitcher, said he knew of another young pitcher who'd had the operation and gained three to five miles an hour on his fastball. "I'm not saying that's the reason to do it," the man told Longman. Yet he said that it was a consideration, telling the reporter, "It's encouraging to think [his son] might get more velocity."

Frank Jobe believes the answer isn't more Tommy John surgeries for children—it's better education for adults. Parents and coaches have a responsibility to keep their young players safe and secure, he tells me. There's no excuse for a child to be pitching until his arm is sore. "You know 'No pain, no gain'?" asks the courtly Jobe. "I'd like to punch the guy who said that."

The Tommy John tendon transplant is far from the only operation performed mostly, or exclusively, to return young athletes to sports. Speaking with surgeons and parents, I learned just how prevalent these specialized operations are becoming. One of the riskiest is an operation designed to heal swimmers with chronic shoulder problems. It's called a capsular shift and is considered a last resort because there are no guarantees about how it will affect a swimmer's stroke. The purpose of the operation is to stabilize the shoulder joint without overly restricting the patient's range of motion. It's no mean trick. The most cogent explanation of why swimmers are plagued with lax shoulders comes from Scott Montgomery and David Diduch, sports medicine physicians at the University of Virginia. They explain that the shoulder joint is like a golf ball on a tee: It can easily fall off. A dislocation means the ball is knocked completely off the tee. Often, it doesn't return to proper realignment without help. In a subluxation, the ball moves partly off the tee. Athletes in contact sports are more prone to dislocations while swimmers are more likely to suffer subluxation. The more they swim, the more lax their shoulder can become. The cycle can greatly reduce their performance.

Brooke Bennett knows all about microtrauma and subluxation. A three-time gold medalist and member of the 1996 and 2000 U.S. Olympic swim teams, Bennett is one of the premier women's freestyle swimmers in American history and one of the best in recent years on the international scene. At the 2000 Summer Games, she set a world record in the 800-meter freestyle competition. Bennett was twenty years old then. She had her sights on qualifying for a third Olympics and had begun training in earnest for the 2004 Summer Games when pain in both of her shoulders forced her out of the pool. In 2001, she underwent bilateral surgery, first for the right shoulder and, a month later, for the left. Months of grueling rehab followed. And then Bennett returned to training, staying on track through the Olympic trials in 2004. Still pain-free, she finished third in the 800-meter freestyle, a performance that must have been both satisfying and cruelly disappointing—only the top two finishers qualified for the U.S. team.

Some sports injuries that are repaired today were undetected or, worse, misdiagnosed only a few decades ago. Such is the case with labral tears of the hip, an injury that can sideline young athletes in sports such as golf, hockey, and soccer. The labrum is a smooth cartilage that runs along the rims of the ball and socket in the hip, creating a tight fit. Sports in which players make frequent stops and starts and change direction suddenly are hard on hips. One result can be small tears or other damage to the labrum. Few surgeons were repairing labral tears until twenty years ago. When the injury was diagnosed properly, the common treatment was to allow the labrum to heal on its own. Later studies suggested that the conservative approach led to problems later on. The frayed labrum disturbed healthy cartilage in the joint, causing many patients to develop arthritis, Dr. Joseph McCarthy, a pioneer in labral tear surgery, told the *Wall Street Journal*. Now arthroscopic hip surgeries are performed on about fifteen thousand patients each year, according to the *Journal*. Using arthroscopy, surgeons insert a small camera and tiny tools through a series of small incisions. The surgery is over in a few hours. That day, athletes begin their recovery. In three months, many athletes are back with their teams.

Some of their patients, like soccer player Gary Weisbaum of Baltimore, are still in high school. "The first time I noticed it, I was kicking a ball with my left foot. I felt a little tweak and didn't think anything of it. I ran off the field and told my father, 'I think I pulled my groin.' For a good six or seven months, I didn't let it stop me. I guess I just got used to it. Eventually, it became too much."

In the fall of 2007, Gary had surgery at the Steadman-Hawkins Clinic in Colorado, a haven for athletes with hip injuries. Four hours after his surgery, he was riding a stationary bike. His rehab progressed rapidly thanks to some cutting-edge rehab devices. One of Gary's favorites was a pair of inflammation-fighting, irrigated shorts. For home-use only, the neoprene pants are equipped with plastic tubing that connects to an ice-filled container and a pump that circulates thirty-seven-degree water over the patient's hip.

"It sounds weird, but it felt great," Gary told me. "I asked my dad if we could keep them." The technology shortened Gary's recovery but at a cost to his parents, Harold and Sharon. All told, the uncovered medical bills and travel expenses approached $15,000. There was no arguing with the results. Three months after the surgery, Gary and his father returned to the Colorado clinic where Gary received an optimistic report: The labral tear repair had healed, and he was cleared to begin rehab of his muscles and ligaments. In 2008, he started his freshman year at the University of New Mexico, where, after several weeks of practice, he suffered the same, unusual injury in his opposite hip.

My son, Ben, hurt his elbow in the third inning, maybe the fourth. In any case, we didn't learn about it until the game was over. He walked to where my wife, Peggy, and I were standing, pointed to his arm, and announced, "It's killing me." They weren't words we were expecting. He had just turned in one of the better performances of his high school baseball life, at just the right time. His team was playing for a berth in the conference championship game. For a school that hadn't been there in ten years, that was big. That May afternoon, Ben didn't throw the most impressive fastballs. In fact, he seemed to be tossing more softly than usual, relying instead on changing speeds of his pitches to confuse hitters. Whatever he did, it worked. The other guys managed five hits. Ben's team won in a walk, 7-0, and punched its ticket to the title game.

My first thought was that Ben had a mild case of tendonitis in his elbow, an echo of the injury he'd suffered several years earlier. A few weeks rest usually was all the therapy needed. I still wasn't overly concerned three days later when the championship game rolled around and the season ended on a somber note—Ben's team lost in a rout. He played third base. And, with his elbow still sore, he could barely negotiate the throw across the infield. A week later, Ben tried throwing again. It hurt. Two weeks later, no improvement.

I called Charles Silberstein, our family orthopedist. We scheduled an appointment to see Chick, as his admirers know him, and several days later were face to face in a small treatment room. He told Ben to take off his shirt. Then, as I watched and listened, he pulled and pushed Ben's elbow until my son groaned. Whatever was wrong with Ben's elbow, it was clear Chick had seen it many times before.

I wasn't prepared for what came next. In a somber, if reassuring, tone, Chick explained that Ben's injury likely was quite serious: a rupture to the ulnar collateral ligament in his right elbow. His physical exam indicated as much. And Ben's symptoms were also classic: a dagger in the inside of his elbow at the moment in throwing when his arm accelerated forward. Dr. Silberstein ordered an MRI to confirm his suspicions. We had the results a few days later. The ligament was damaged.

I found a helpful explanation of UCL injuries in a patient guide prepared by Johns Hopkins Sports Medicine. It helped me picture what had gone wrong in Ben's elbow. "The best way to think of a ligament is as a tether between the bones, which gets too tight when the bones move. When a ligament is torn, the tether is too long and the bones move too much. This can lead to pain, a sense of instability or looseness, and inability to work or do your sport. The ulnar collateral ligament (UCL) is located on the inside of the elbow (small finger side of the arm). The UCL attaches on one side to the humerus (the bone of the upper arm) and on the other to the ulna (a bone in the forearm). The largest stresses in the elbow are those forces that cause twisting and bending of the elbow. These motions put extreme stress on the ligament during certain parts of the motion."

I was in a state of deep surprise, though I had no right. The risk factors for UCL injuries in baseball players include flawed mechanics, muscle imbalances, and too much throwing. All were present in Ben's pitching. We learned about the first two later on. The last was my burden to carry.

What had I done to protect Ben from throwing too many

baseballs? Not nearly enough. Each year his season expanded and I did not object. The high school season began with February workouts and ended in mid-May. At fifteen, he wanted to play in a summer league for a coach we both respect. That doubled the length of the season. Then came an invitation to play with teammates from his school in a fall league. Now, with a few breaks, it was baseball from February until almost November.

As I had years before, his coaches asked a lot of his arm. I was mostly complicit. I didn't want to make waves. Besides, I *wanted* him to pitch. Only once can I remember putting up even the mildest protest: It was the first weekend of the season, when players are gaining strength in their arms. Ben's coach used him as a pitcher and catcher in a doubleheader, prompting me to send a concerned e-mail. I felt uneasy doing even that. But I did it. I had the same queasy feeling toward the end of Ben's senior season in high school just before his elbow called it quits. The games were coming fast and furious: six in eight or nine days. The schedulers had put the coaches of Ben's team, and all the others, in an impossible position. In the deluge of games, they couldn't possibly give their pitchers proper rest. Ben was probably no more or less pooped than the others. It was impossible to know whether the workload was a large factor or no factor at all in his injury. At that point, it didn't much matter.

Dr. Silberstein explained Ben's options. He could forget about baseball. Just give it up. Ben didn't take that one seriously. If he was intent on playing again, there were two paths to choose from. The first, which the doctor favored, was to spend the next eight weeks trying to rehabilitate the elbow. Even if Ben followed the program to the letter, the ligament would never heal completely. And Ben's old strength would not fully return. But by strengthening the surrounding muscles, Ben might steal back, say, 75 percent of his old self. The other choice required an operation and afterward an arduous year-long recovery: Tommy John surgery.

Ben wanted the surgery. My guess was that he would have

stripped off his shirt and lain down on the operating table right away without anesthesia if necessary. He wanted to play baseball again the way he had before, without restrictions. That was ambitious. We urged Ben to try rehab. His elbow might respond well, allowing him to regain more of his old self than he thought possible. In other words, he might surprise himself. The program that was mapped out consisted of two main components: exercises to strengthen healthy muscles in his arm and regular throwing sessions. Therapy was full-time. He had several appointments a week with a physical therapist experienced in treating UCL injuries. At home, elastic therapy bands popped up, knotted to banisters and doorknobs. Ben dutifully used them, flexing and unflexing his right arm at all hours. His throwing regimen started with games of catch at a very short distance, twenty feet. The next week, he'd move back to thirty feet, then forty-five and so on until he was almost as far away from me as a center fielder stands from home plate.

Ben kept up the throwing program when it would have been understandable to quit or at least pause. His rehab assignment overlapped with an eleven-day Baltic cruise, a step up from our usual family vacations. He did not miss a single throwing day. We played catch on deck during a North Sea passage and had games of long toss in Copenhagen and Helsinki, where I heard an American tourist marveling at how at long last the national pastime finally was catching on in Finland. For a few days the pain would subside. Then it would be back with a wallop, bad as ever.

Peggy and I weren't opposed to Ben having Tommy John surgery. We were opposed to surgery with no apparent purpose. Ben's damaged elbow did not qualify as your typical disability. True, he could not throw a baseball without pain. We were told he would be unable to throw a javelin in his condition either. Otherwise, living with a ruptured UCL is quite uninhibiting. There's almost nothing a person with the injury cannot do. For the rest of his life, Ben would be able to carry groceries, mow lawns, and move grand pianos. If he chose to throw a baseball softly or at short distances, he could do that, too. The only limitation would be pain. He wouldn't have to worry about letting one rip and doing more damage to his arm. With his injury, that wasn't possible.

Then why would someone in Ben's position undergo Tommy John surgery? Years earlier, for a *BusinessWeek* article, I had asked that very question of Lewis Yocum. The surgeon's words echoed back now. He'd told me that operating on a teenager who might play a handful of high school or college games and be forced to give up the sport after a year of difficult rehabilitation made little sense. "Just because we have a hammer doesn't mean everything is a nail," Yocum had said. "Obviously, the surgery isn't designed for everybody." I'd been quick to judge the parents of Yocum's young patients—harshly, it seemed, all these years later. Now I was standing in their shoes.

I couldn't figure out where Ben would play baseball. By now, he had started his freshman year at George Washington University in Washington, D.C., a highly regarded school with all the academic programs and city life he was looking for. GW also has a top-notch Division I athletics program. The baseball team recruited players who had been stars on high school teams throughout the Northeast. Ben had willed and worked himself into a capable player in high school and, in his senior year, earned a place on the local all-conference team. He'd never competed against gifted athletes like the ones at GW. Anything was possible with someone as single-minded as Ben. He might transform himself into a Division I baseball player after all. But unless the plan included transplanting Tommy John's own ligament into my son's elbow, I didn't see how. That was on Mondays. Tuesdays, I was daydreaming again, imagining Ben firing fastballs and being carried off the field on the shoulders of his GW teammates. (In some versions of the fantasy, I was interviewed by *Sports Illustrated*.) I knew I shouldn't be thinking this way. I tried not to. Really.

Peggy and I left the decision to Ben. It made sense that his vote be the tiebreaker. It was his elbow and his future. It was his call for another reason. At eighteen, he was a legal adult. If he was hell-bent on having Tommy John surgery, he could do so without our permission. Though there was the small matter of health insurance. Without his parents' coverage, he would have been hard-pressed to pay the $15,000 bill. (Yes, Tommy John surgery is a covered medical expense.)

In October, the three of us sat down around the dinner table for a long-awaited family meeting. Peggy and I knew Ben's thinking. That had never been in doubt. Before a decision was made, we wanted to give our appraisals. Peggy spoke first. She said the operation was rough stuff. A year earlier, Ben had two wisdom teeth extracted. He sailed through the surgery. "Think about having twenty removed at once," she said. She talked about all that would come after surgery: slings, casts, and months of physical therapy. While the operation's success rate was very high (93 percent of patients pitch again), he'd have to work hard to get his old elbow back. "You can do it," she told him. "Do you *want* to?"

When it was my turn, I asked one question. "If you don't make the GW team, will you feel the surgery was a waste?"

Ben's views hadn't changed since Chick Silberstein broke the news of his injury in May. "If I don't make the team, I'll be fine," he said. "If I don't have the surgery, and never know if I could have made the team, I won't be fine with that."

Ben surprised us with another thought, one that further boosted our confidence. It also made me smile. He recalled the silly baseball games we played in the front yard when he and Eli were little boys—Wiffle ball, the "fly ball game," all totally improvised and so much fun. Each required a dad able to lift his arm above his shoulder and throw ninety feet across our yard. And a dad able to do it again and again until it was too dark to see. If he ever had kids, Ben told us, he wanted to be that dad.

On December 11, 2006, Ben and I sat in the second-floor orthopedics offices of Johns Hopkins at Green Spring Station, a suburban branch of the main hospital. His surgery was in eleven days. This was the final pre-op appointment, a last chance to quiz Ben's surgeon about what to expect and what to feverishly put out of our minds. We sat in treatment room 3, furnished with the tools of modern orthopedics: a sink, an examination table, a hand sanitizer, and, resting on a counter between us, a skeletal elbow. For a few minutes, Ben and I made small talk, trying to ease our anxiety and not succeeding, when the door opened and in walked Dr. Andrew Cosgarea. Our friend Chick Silberstein had finally retired from the operating room, and Cosgarea was his replacement as Baltimore's orthopedic surgeon to the stars. Cosgarea cared for the Baltimore Orioles, Johns Hopkins athletes in a dozen sports, and now Ben Hyman. A trim, athletic man, Cosgarea attended Penn State on a swimming scholarship. He's a rabid Bruce Springsteen fan. He smiled and made introductions. He gave Ben a brief medical exam, pulling and probing his elbow much as Chick had. Then he sat down between Ben and me.

The three of us had our eyes on the medical file that Cosgarea carried into the room. There were white, pink, and yellow forms inside. Cosgarea pulled out one with the heading *Consent for Performance of Operations or other Procedures*. He jotted "right elbow" on the paper and circled the words. He looked at Ben and waited for Ben to look back. For the next five minutes, Cosgarea explained the surgery in all the detail Ben wanted and perhaps more. When he was through, he asked if Ben had questions. My son had been waiting for this chance.

How long would the operation last?

About two hours.

Would he be in pain afterward?

Yes, but there was medication for that.

How long would he be in a brace?

Five weeks.

Would he be able to go to a baseball camp in Florida to be a counselor one week after surgery?

Seriously, Ben.

Dr. Cosgarea read aloud the various disclaimers on the consent form and paused before sharing the paragraph that enumerated the list of things that could happen during any major operation, this one included: chance of damage to arteries or nerves, blood clots, stroke, and death. I doubt Ben had considered the possibility, however remote, that getting his fastball back could be fatal. He reached for a pen and without comment signed the form.

On December 22, my wife and I, with Ben bundled in his GW baseball jacket in the back seat, were in the car and headed to Johns Hopkins Hospital by five a.m. Ben was Cosgarea's first patient, scheduled for seven thirty. After saying good-bye in the waiting room, we saw Ben once before surgery—in a pre-op area where he had changed into a surgical patient—wearing his hospital gown and hairnet. Cosgarea visited briefly and, with a purple indelible marker in his hand, jotted notes to himself on the inside of Ben's elbows. On the left, he scribbled, NO. On the right, YES, and below, his initials, AJC.

That was the last we saw of Ben for several hours. Within minutes, he lay on his back in a chilly operating room, attended by eight figures in scrubs and surgical masks—nurses, anesthesiologists, a surgical resident, a physician's assistant, and Cosgarea. When the anesthesia kicked in, the operation began. Cosgarea made a deep horizontal incision along the inside of Ben's right elbow, exposing the ligament. The surgeon checked to see that the ligament was indeed damaged. Then he shifted his focus below the elbow; he made two small incisions and removed the palmaris longus, a length of a tendon running to Ben's wrist. Cosgarea placed the disembodied tendon—the graft to be used in reconstructing Ben's elbow—on a moist sponge.

Now was the time for power tools, a gruesome necessity in every Tommy John operation. With a high-speed burr, Cosgarea carefully drilled a series of small tunnels in the bones of Ben's upper and lower arms. Then he reached for the newly harvested tendon, threading the graft through the newly drilled holes in the bones as if lacing a shoe. He sewed up the wound and let down the tourniquet that had kept blood from pulsing through Ben's arm. The surgery was over in just under two hours.

Just after nine-thirty, Cosgarea appeared in the waiting room, still in his green scrubs, well into a full day of repairing rotator cuffs and meniscus tears. Ben had done well, he told us. No complications. We could go see him in recovery. The room was bright and busy, with patients in recliners, dozing and sipping from cans of ginger ale. Ben was groggy, mixed up, lucid and chatty all at the same time. His right arm was encased in plaster from his shoulder to his knuckles; his fingers were a disturbing cast of whitish yellow. He said he felt pins and needles at the fingertips, an aftereffect of the tourniquet. Above all, like his parents, he was relieved.

7   RISKING EVERYTHING

Kimiko Hirai is open about her past. As a college student and Olympic diver, she suffered from bulimia, a debilitating eating disorder in which sufferers are caught in an endless cycle of binge eating followed by behavior referred to as purging. Typically, they get rid of food by vomiting. Sometimes, bulimics resort to laxatives, enemas, and even fasting.

For almost two years, Hirai lived through hell. She was controlled by thoughts of food, of when to eat and how to purge what she'd eaten. Like other bulimics, wherever she was going, she knew exactly where to buy laxatives and the location of the bathrooms. She plotted strategy about slipping away from friends and coaches so that she could empty her stomach. Fears about gaining weight were all-consuming. In a shopping mall, she chose stairs instead of escalators, thinking, "Maybe I can burn one more calorie." She could not put a stick of gum in her mouth without worrying about the five calories she would be ingesting.

A member of the 2004 U.S. Olympic team, Hirai traces her eating ordeal to her first days as a college athlete at Indiana University. She was at risk, she believes, for the same reasons so many female athletes are. She was driven to succeed in her sport, and she was a self-described pleaser. She craved approval from her teammates and her coaches. Especially her coaches. She recalls a brief exchange with a coach the summer before she began classes at Indiana. She asked the coach what she could do to prepare for the start of diving workouts in the fall. Hirai has no trouble remembering the coach's response: "Don't get fat." Later, after school had begun and Hirai had slipped into a cycle of eating and purging, the coach raised the issue of food again. During a meeting with the entire team, the subject of eating disorders came up, and, Hirai recalls, the coach turned to her. "I still don't know whether it was tongue-in-cheek. But he said, 'You're not doing any of that crap, are you?'" The incident left her feeling shamed and more isolated than ever. "I decided right there I was never going to tell him what I was doing."

For the next eighteen months, she purged almost everything. Her weight plunged from 130 pounds to 100, a precipitous loss. She sought help for her eating disorder only after graduating from Indiana and, she says, pulling away from negative influences there. From a distance of more than a decade, Hirai sees her experience with a clarity that escaped her in her diving days. She accepts responsibility for her bulimia, for what she did to her body, and why. "It's easy to point and blame. I won't do that," she says. Yet the attitudes of coaches "absolutely contributed" to her eating disorders, Hirai told me. "Coaches carry tremendous power, whether they realize it or not, whether they like it or not," she says. "People with eating disorders are people pleasers. When you tell me, 'Don't get fat,' when that's your number one thing, I'm going to do everything I can to make you happy. Not only that, I'm going to lose twenty pounds, and you're going to be more pleased and really like me."

In the high-stakes world of youth sports, the most troubling and least understood injuries may be the ones that are self-inflicted. The list is a compendium of disorders, syndromes, and risky behaviors that target our children, often the most talented and driven. The list is scary: anabolic steroids that build astonishing muscle mass but leave users with damaging lifelong health effects; brain injuries resulting from multiple concussions; and eating disorders that shrink some young athletes and dangerously bulk up others. Why are children literally putting their lives at risk in pursuit of sports glory? Many reasons, of course. Pressure from peers. A child's in-born curiosity, even recklessness. Too often, youth athletes have unwitting accomplices—coaches and parents.

Hirai's story ends happily. Though she failed to win an Olympic medal in 2004, she retired from diving content with her career. She married a diving coach, Purdue's Adam Soldati, and the couple has a young son. Her marriage to a diving coach even has tempered resentments about her own coaches.

Hirai's struggle is not unusual. Cathy Rigby, the Olympic gymnast of the 1960s, and Zina Garrison, a Wimbledon doubles champ, have acknowledged lengthy battles with bulimia. So has Carling Bassett-Seguso, whose eating disorder derailed a promising tennis career in the 1980s. Bassett seemed to have it all: a strong game that propelled her to the number eight spot in world rankings and blond good looks that made her one of the most ogled athletes of her day. Behind the glamorous façade, she was barely coping. Boys, puberty, the pressure of tennis, and a fledgling career as a fashion model took a toll. When she was sixteen years old, another tennis pro showed her how she put her fingers down her throat and purged. Soon Bassett was throwing up eighteen to twenty times *a day*. Her weight slid from 125 pounds to 96. She left the tour having accomplished little that was predicted for her. Not until her first pregnancy did she seek help. That was twenty years ago. Now Bassett-Seguso and her husband, former tennis pro Robert Seguso, have two sons and a daughter, all talented tennis players, all healthy eaters. She fears some of today's top pros are not, and she has spoken up about players whom she feels show signs of a problem.

■ ■ ■

Jenny had a healthy attitude about food and her body until she became a cheerleader in college. The experience was one of the most destructive in her life. She cut back to two meals a day, eating only salads and low-calorie cereals. She took diet pills. At times she exercised three times a day. Now in her thirties, she is in therapy but, for now, free of her dysfunctional eating habits. She still worries about her anorexia and bulimia returning. As a cheerleader, Jenny, who spoke with me on the condition that I not reveal her last name, says she was sucked into an appearance-driven culture unlike anything she had known. Her teammates weighed themselves constantly and, when they weren't doing that, compared suntans. Her coach was an even more destructive influence. Jenny remembers belittling comments about her weight, including some that still sting. Once, she says, the coach told her, "Do you realize we have to order a bigger [uniform] size for you than any of the other girls?" At her parents' urging, Jenny quit the squad after one season. Lately, she says, she has been able to look back and draw lessons from the experience. One is to leave behind "toxic people" like her former coach. "They will only make you feel dissatisfied, no matter how much weight you lose," she says.

There are many points of connection in the stories of Kimiko Hirai, Carling Bassett-Seguso, and other athletes struggling with eating disorders. One is that they're focused on getting to the top of their insanely competitive sports. Athletes in so-called thin-build sports such as running, swimming, figure skating, and diving are eager to measure up to the expectations of adults around them.

And there's another connection: often they're women. Eating disorders are distressingly common among female players, especially those who reach the highest rungs. In a study of Division I college athletes, one third of women reported attitudes and symptoms placing them at risk for anorexia nervosa. But male athletes aren't immune. In sports in which maximum performance and ideal body weight are linked—crew, bodybuilding, running, wrestling, and football—they are, in fact, just as vulnerable as the female athletes.

For boys, the pressure to shed weight, and to shed it quickly, may be most intense in wrestling. Training often focuses on "dropping down," shorthand for doing whatever is necessary to slip into a lower, more advantageous, weight class. The most ambitious wrestlers can lose ten to fifteen pounds in a matter of days, sticking to a maniacal regimen, which includes restricting food and drink, loading up on laxatives, and sweating it out in saunas. The risk was never more evident than in 1997. In little more than a month, three college wrestlers died while on crash weight-loss programs. Within a few months, the NCAA had issued stringent rules regarding weight loss, banning the use of rubber suits, diuretics for any reason, and saunas for water loss.

The deprivation that typifies the fatal cases is hard to fathom. One of those who died, Jeffrey Reese, a junior at the University of Michigan, had set a goal of losing twenty-two pounds in just four days. To accomplish it, he put himself through pure torture. Reese limited his diet to fruit and water-based foods. All the while, he exercised relentlessly and insanely, riding a stationary bicycle in a sauna while wearing a rubber suit. At the moment Reese's heart stopped, almost unbelievably, the wrestler had been checking his weight on a scale, according to the *Michigan Daily,* the campus newspaper.

The risky mindset isn't limited to college wrestling, where scholarships and campus glory are at stake, or even high school wrestling. Sometimes the young athletes skipping breakfast and lunch are kindergarteners. Yes, five-year-olds are "cutting weight," with the encouragement of parents.

Young Bennie was a spunky wrestler from a family steeped in wrestling tradition. His story was documented by two Ohio physicians, Randy Sansone and Robert Sawyer, and published in the *British Journal of Sports Medicine* in 2005. Bennie's father had been modestly successful during his days on the mat, and an older son, fifteen, had followed his dad's footsteps in the sport, even winning recognition on the national level. The father clearly had a deep emotional investment in his sons' wrestling activities and attended every one of their matches.

Bennie was preparing for the season finale, a little-guy wrestling championship on which much was riding for the boy and, apparently, much more for his father. On the day of weigh-ins—when wrestlers step on scales to determine their wrestling classification—the team coach heard the boy chiding teammates about their food intake. As the coach listened, Bennie went on, telling other wrestlers, "I'll bet that I was the only one in the sauna last night. I haven't had anything to eat today, or yesterday."

The astonished coach couldn't believe he was listening to a five-year-old. As he thought about the boy, his father, and the upcoming match, the pieces fit together. The boy had been on the cusp of wrestling in a weight class lower than his usual class, and there were reasons for the highly ambitious father to push his son. Bennie had been victorious in all but one of his matches during the season. If he were able to compete at the lower weight in the final match, he would avoid a rematch against the only tyke who'd beaten him. When the coach contacted the father, he admitted he'd gone too far but explained his reasons: He was helping his son uphold the family's wrestling reputation.

Bennie was too young to object. But some athletes fight back. There is, in fact, at least one lawsuit in which the defendant is a coach alleged to have caused one of his players to suffer an eating disorder. Jennifer Besler sued her former high school basketball coach at a New Jersey high school and temporarily won $1.5 million. Besler told a jury that she suffered an eating disorder and stopped menstruating after her former coach, Daniel Hussong, insisted she lose ten pounds. In her lawsuit, Besler claimed the coach belittled her mercilessly, spewed obscenities, and created an intensely stressful environment. A jury agreed, finding the school district liable for emotional distress and awarding Besler a $1.5 million judgment.

On appeal, Besler's victory vanished. (A judge ruled that she'd failed to prove her injuries were permanent, as required under New Jersey law.)

For another population of dedicated youth athletes, the health risks come not from pressure to lose weight but to pack on the pounds. Obesity is the objective for these athletes, most often football players on the offensive and defensive lines. A high school lineman who can crank up his body weight to 270 pounds and manhandle smaller, lighter opponents is a coach's dream. Those who possess above-average speed and quickness to go with their girth are even more prized; they're assured of knocks on the door from college coaches breathlessly waving scholarship offers. Such players are even grist for *New York Times* bestsellers. Michael Lewis's 2006 book, *The Blind Side,* recounts the life story of 344-pound Michael Oher of Memphis, who was just about his city's hottest attraction since Elvis. Oher's huge load, matched with impressive athletic skills, turned out to be prized credentials. They delivered the African American youth from a broken home in the inner city to admission to one of the city's toniest, and whitest, prep schools. From there, he went on to become a college football star at Ole Miss.

A body that's built as a human wrecking ball isn't necessarily a healthy body. In 2005, researchers at the University of North Carolina-Chapel Hill studied the vital statistics of NFL players and determined that 56 percent of the league's 2,168 players counted were obese. The health consequences for that group are uncertain. But people who carry excessive weight are known to be at higher risk for a variety of maladies, from high blood pressure to heart disease to sleep disorders. One study published in the *New England Journal of Medicine* connects the dots in ways that should alarm every past and present NFL player. Its findings include this: 34

percent of linemen suffer from sleep apnea, a temporary ces-
sation of respiration caused when breathing passages close.
(In the general population, the percentage is 4 percent.) The
death of NFL lineman Reggie White has been blamed in
part on sleep apnea. White was just forty-three when he died.
The life expectancy of the average American is 77.6 years.
According to recent studies, it's 55 years for NFL players
generally and 52 for linemen.

The collective, coast-to-coast bulking up of college and
even high school football players is hardly a secret to parents
and coaches. It shouldn't be to any who have their eyes open.
Such players, after all, are hard to miss. And there are plenty
of them. A study of more than 3,600 high school linemen in
Iowa discovered that 45 percent were overweight and 9 percent of those were obese, according to research published in
the *Journal of the American Medical Association* in 2007.

The problem is as critical among even younger players.
Of 653 players, ages nine to fourteen, playing youth football
in Michigan, 45 percent are overweight or obese, according to a study published in the *Journal of Pediatrics* in 2007.
Robert M. Malina, one of the study's authors, told the *New
York Times,* "Youngsters are being rewarded for being big and
overweight before playing big-time football."

Players seeking to bulk up can find all the help they need in
weight rooms or—for those in a hurry—at health-food stores.
It couldn't be easier. They plunk down their money for Muscle Milk, Muscle Tech, or other physique-enhancing dietary
supplements—each one perfectly legal.

Those over-the-counter products are especially worrisome
to physicians. Creatine, for example, is one of the most widely
available and popular supplements—by some estimates, sales
each year top $400 million. The human body takes in cre-
atine through protein-rich foods like meat and fish, then, in
a process better left to endocrinologists to explain, converts
it into the energy we use while running, jumping, or swimming—any sort of high-intensity aerobic exercise. Creatine

that comes in a jar just adds to those natural stores and, proponents claim, shortens recovery time, increases endurance, and helps athletes quickly add weight and muscle.

Of greatest concern about creatine is what doctors *don't* understand about its health effects, which, pertaining to use by young athletes, is plenty. There are no studies of creatine use by children under age eighteen, and little is known about its long-term effects on young bodies. (Several cases of kidney failure in adults have been linked to creatine use.) Yet in spite of that research gap, the supplement is being used by young athletes. Nearly 6 percent of youth athletes in grades six through twelve had either used or were using creatine, according to one study published in the medical journal *Pediatrics* in 2001. Creatine was used most by athletes in football, wrestling, ice hockey, gymnastics, and lacrosse. The most common reasons given for taking the supplement were "enhanced performance" and "improved appearance."

Pediatricians Carla Laos and Jordan Metzl attribute the troubling use of creatine to one more factor: overly invested adults pushing their children to achieve more. "Young athletes are under tremendous pressure from parents, coaches, and peers to succeed in sports. This win-at-all-costs mentality may contribute to the temptation to use not only creatine, but also other performance-enhancing drugs," Laos and Metzl write.

Among illegal drugs, the most problematic are anabolic steroids, miracle muscle-builders that have become synonymous with bad behavior in professional and amateur sports. Canadian sprinter Ben Johnson was the first high-profile casualty of a steroid scandal. After winning the 100-meter sprint at the 1988 Summer Olympics in Seoul, defeating the American favorite Carl Lewis, Johnson was caught using the anabolic steroid Stanozolol and stripped of his gold medal. In the decades since, Johnson hasn't come close to a gold medal for contrition. In 2006, he claimed that "40 percent of people in sports are still using performance[-enhancing drugs]." Johnson turned out to be on the leading edge of the performance-enhancing revolution in professional sports. In the past two decades, a former NFL player, Lyle Alzado, blamed prolonged steroid abuse for the cancer that eventually killed him. Barry Bonds's home run record is clouded by his alleged use of "the clear and the cream." And American Floyd Landis was stripped of the Tour de France championship after testing showed abnormally high levels of testosterone. Doping has become so pervasive in professional sports that even the august ladies and men's professional golf tours, paragons of sportsmanship, have felt the need to keep pro golfers clean with drug-testing programs.

Anabolic steroids aren't just a dangerous shortcut for adults. Of an estimated 3 million people in the United States using the illicit drugs, one in four admits starting as a teenager. The number of young steroid users today is unclear. In Southern California, only 1 percent of high school students acknowledge they've used steroids, but they claim that 10 percent of athletes at their school are users, according to a 2007 study by the LA84 Foundation. Other studies show steroid use on the rise. High school students who admitted to steroid use nearly doubled to 6.1 percent in 2003, from 3.1 percent in 1998, according to the Centers for Disease Control and Prevention.

These statistics, however imprecise, are terrifying. Anabolic steroids are man-made substances that mimic the effects of testosterone. In boys, large doses of steroids can signal the body to stop making testosterone. That stops bones from growing because the body is tricked into believing it has reached full development. If a young male athlete stops taking steroids and can't produce more of his own testosterone, he is at risk of developing feminine characteristics, such as breasts or a speaking voice octaves too high. Long-term abusers face greater risks: heart disease and cancer of the prostate and liver.

The war on steroids has been slower to reach youth athletes. In 2007, only Texas, Florida, and New Jersey had mandatory drug-testing programs for high school athletes.

Illinois expects to begin limited drug testing of athletes soon, and no doubt other states will follow. Even in these trailblazing places, however, a teenager would stand a better chance of getting a perfect score on her SAT than of being lined up for a drug screening. Early protocols were ridiculously selective, with a tiny fraction of athletes tested: 1 percent of wrestlers and football and baseball players in Florida; 3 percent of 740,000 public high school athletes in Texas; 5 percent of athletes competing in championship tournaments in New Jersey (about five hundred of the state's 230,000 high school athletes). In their first years, at least, such programs are hardly uncovering nests of steroid abuse. During the 2006–2007 school year, New Jersey's drug testing found one athlete who tested positive for a performance-enhancing drug.

Governments have reason for moving at a glacial pace. Mandatory testing is a nightmare to administer, has been opposed by the American Civil Liberties Union, among other rights organizations, and, perhaps most significantly, is very expensive. In the first cycle of testing in New Jersey, officials said the cost to the state of testing five hundred players was about $50,000. Likewise, the Texas program, which cost the state $6 million a year, has been criticized in newspaper editorials across the state as "ill conceived" and "nearly impossible to monitor."

Yet the alternatives to testing programs that cost too much and catch few drug abusers are even less acceptable. Don Hooton of Plano, Texas, was one of the ad hoc lobbyists who pushed hard in his state for a high school drug-testing plan. He did it for his son, Taylor, who would be in his early twenties—if he had lived. Taylor died one month past his seventeenth birthday. On July 15, 2003, the high school pitcher went in his bedroom, closed the door, and hanged himself. Don Hooton believes anabolic steroids killed his son, if not directly, then directly enough. For months before his death, Taylor had been suffering a clinical depression that Don Hooton thinks was triggered by the use of, and withdrawal from, illicit drugs. As early as the 1990s, the American Academy of Pediatrics warned that mood swings and depression were known side effects of anabolic steroid use in children.

Until Taylor's death, Don and his wife, Gwen, had been in the dark about their son's use of anabolic steroids. So had Taylor's high school baseball coaches. There's an awful lesson in that. And there is another in the life and death of Taylor Hooton, this one about the power and influence of adults in the lives of young athletes. Taylor began taking steroids during his junior year at Plano West Senior High School, outside Dallas. Don Hooton can almost pinpoint the day. As for the reason, he explains, "We don't need to speculate about that. We know."

Don Hooton is referring to a conversation, a fleeting few words, really, between his son, a promising pitcher on the JV squad, and the JV coach. As Don Hooton tells it, Taylor was coming off the field one afternoon when the coach intercepted him, telling him that if he planned to play varsity next season, he needed to "get bigger." Baseball was in Taylor Hooton's head and in his blood. His older brother, Donald, was a Division I college pitcher in Louisiana. His cousin Burt Hooton is a former major league pitcher with the Los Angeles Dodgers. Like Kimiko Hirai, Taylor Hooton was determined to please his coach, and then some. Don Hooton says the psychiatrist who treated his son for depression told him that Taylor had explained why he began taking steroids, and that Taylor had referred to the coach's comment about needing to get bigger. And, Don Hooton explained, Taylor suspected that other players were using steroids, too.

Taylor, already nearly six-foot-two and a solid 175 pounds, bulked up to 205. Don took that as a sign that his son was working out diligently. Taylor developed a severe case of acne on his back and became irritable and quick to anger, classic signs of steroid use. His parents insisted that he be tested for drugs, but the test that was given, they learned later, was one that didn't detect steroids.

Don Hooton believes that his son had stopped taking steroids in the months before his death. He had been injecting himself with the steroid Decca 300 and taking another steroid, Anadrol, orally. After he died, a sweep of Taylor's bedroom by Don Hooton and police produced vials of steroids, syringes, and needles. Don Hooton says the drugs came from a nineteen-year-old dealer, whom his son met while working out at the local YMCA. Consider it a cautionary tale, says the father. "Don't assume any place is safe."

These days, Don Hooton, a telecom executive, devotes much of his time to the Taylor Hooton Foundation for Fighting Steroid Abuse, a nonprofit he and his wife established in 2004. He travels the country speaking to parents, coaches, and state legislatures about steroid abuse, and he has testified before Congress three times. When Senator George Mitchell released his bombshell report on performance-enhancing drug use in Major League Baseball, he mentioned the Taylor Hooton tragedy at the press conference.

Don Hooton remains furious with the coach of his son's high school team for making an offhand remark to Taylor about his physical stature. "What the hell are you telling a kid that big that he needs to get bigger to throw a baseball?" Hooton told me. "We are turning over our sixteen-year-old babies to coaches who are untrained. That really gets to the heart of the matter." Yet he does not blame that coach or other coaches at Plano West Senior High School for Taylor's death. Nor does he blame himself. Four years after Taylor's death, Hooton says the decision to use steroids was his son's. "Ultimately, it is Taylor's fault," he says. Yet, as well as anyone can, he also understands the power of coaches over impressionable, eager-to-please young athletes. "I travel throughout the country [speaking about steroid use], and I hear many stories. If there's a common thread about these situations, it's an instruction these kids are hearing from their coaches: Get bigger."

■ ■ ■

Different from the steroids threat, though no less alarming, are the dangers to youth athletes posed by concussions. Sixty thousand high school athletes suffer concussions of some severity each year. In sports in which players use their heads for more than outsmarting opponents, they are a distressing fact of life. Football, girls soccer, and boys soccer are the top three sports for concussions. In one study of high school football in Wisconsin, 15 percent of players reported sustaining a concussion during the most recent football season; the percentage of players who said they'd had at least one concussion in their lives was nearly double that.

There aren't many youth players who volunteer for the skull-rattling hits that cause concussions. They do everything they can to avoid them. Certainly, youth players and their coaches are better educated to the heath risks of concussions than ever before. That awareness has improved considerably in recent years, thanks in part to Alan Schwarz of the *New York Times,* who has reported extensively on the subject.

In 2006, Schwarz told the tragic story of Will Benson, an ambitious student and star quarterback for St. Stephen's Episcopal School in Austin, Texas. In 2002, Benson was leading the St. Stephens offense in the first game of the season when a jarring head-on tackle stopped him cold. The smack of helmets echoed in the grandstands. Benson quickly regained his feet and played the rest of the game. The first signs of trouble appeared several days later when Benson complained of a headache. As a precaution, he sat out the team's next game. But the following Friday night, he returned to the St. Stephens lineup more concerned about his team's winless record than his brain.

Late in the first half, Benson turned away from his teammates, lifted his helmet, and walked off the field. He told his coach that he saw "big blobs." A few minutes later, in the locker room, he lost consciousness. Five days later, Will Benson died from what doctors described as second-impact syndrome, a condition in which the brain suffers a second, fatal blow before an earlier injury is permitted time to heal. He was seventeen years old.

Though examples of concussion-related deaths are rare, they cause special concern for younger athletes. A study in 2007 of football players found that high school players are at three times greater risk than college players of catastrophic head injuries, suggesting that younger brains are more vulnerable to brain injuries. A 2008 study published in the *Journal of Athletic Training* reached a similar conclusion, that younger adolescents who suffered concussions experience more pronounced deficits in verbal and visual memory than older victims. Given those risks, and the tragic deaths of otherwise healthy young men like Will Benson, you would think youth players would be on alert, hyperaware of the first symptoms of concussions and quick to point them out to coaches and team doctors. On high school football and soccer fields across America, the reality is just the opposite. By and large, youth athletes are perfectly willing to ignore the dangers of concussions and quite literally take their lives in their hands.

Several studies have confirmed as much, including a fascinating one on unreported concussions among high school football players, conducted by researchers Michael McCrea and Kevin Guskiewicz. Canvassing 1,532 high school football players at twenty different high schools in Wisconsin, McCrea and Guskiewicz zeroed in on those who'd been blasted in the head during football games; suffered headaches, dizziness, and blurry vision; and—vital to their research—decided not to tell a coach, parent, or trainer. The findings underscore how massive the mind shift needs to be to protect young players.

More than half the players who'd withheld information about a concussion said they didn't realize that the headache or dizziness they felt after a monstrous hit was so serious that they ought to report it. The next most cited reason was more troubling. Forty-one percent of the Wisconsin boys told Mc-Crea and Guskiewicz that they chose not to tell because, if they shared information with a coach or trainer, they'd likely be taken out of the game.

What the Wisconsin study doesn't explain is whether the parents and coaches of high school athletes in some way help to shape such reckless thinking. Are adults sending messages, subtly or otherwise, that winning comes first and guarding the health of high school players second? Do youth players fear that they have to choose between listening to their bodies and satisfying their coaches and parents?

In his *New York Times* piece, Schwarz addresses these questions with powerful reporting. A physician at a Connecticut high school recalls sending a player from an opposing team to the sidelines with a concussion. The coach then instructed the player to switch his uniform number and surreptitiously return to the game. A team doctor in Charlottesville, Virginia, laments the recklessness of parents who will not listen to any advice that takes their child out of a game. "I have had parents tear up the form that I've filled out strongly recommending their child not play, and shop a doc to get their kid okayed," he says.

Then there is the story of a quarterback from a Memphis high school who, with considerable pride, explains that he once refused to come out of a game after a blow to the head resulted in a concussion. He stayed in the game even though his vision was so blurry he could barely see his receivers. "I couldn't come out—my team needed me," he says. "You have to keep playing until you can't."

8   I'M ANGRY. ARE YOU?

Saturdays in Montgomery County, Maryland, are like Saturdays most everywhere in America. Adults crowd around athletic fields to watch their kids play soccer. They bring grande lattes and their home-delivered editions of the *Washington Post*. Though it's tough to see, they also lug a heavy load of parental emotion. Jay Goldstein has made a career of studying that.

Goldstein's interest is purely academic. A research assistant in the department of kinesiology at the University of Maryland, he studies emotions percolating on sidelines and in bleachers during youth sports games. For his master's thesis, Goldstein came up with a clever idea for a study. He rounded up 340 parents, suburban, college-educated, upper-middle-class Gen-Xers who had children who played sports. After they'd watched their kids run around, score goals, let in goals, play well, not play well, win games, or lose games, Goldstein and his fellow researchers pulled them aside to pass out questionnaires and ask questions. None of them would have anything to do with the game that had just transpired. Goldstein didn't care that much. His research focused on what parents were feeling. Were they angry?

In 2005, Goldstein and Seppo E. Iso-Ahola, a cohort at the University of Maryland, published their study. It suggested something quite fascinating. Youth soccer games tick off a lot of people. Goldstein found that 53 percent of parents reported being angry during games to some degree. You couldn't generalize on what got under their skin because almost everything did. The most frequently cited irritants were referees (35 percent) and, yes, their own child or their child's team (28 percent).

Goldstein won a prestigious award for his research, which for all its simplicity is very revealing. In a sense, it turns conventional wisdom on its head. Shouldn't parents at youth sports games actually be enjoying themselves? Goldstein will tell you that the actual percentage of perturbed adults is probably a good deal higher than even his study indicates. "I would term it the tip of the iceberg," he says. "If you could hook people up and actually measure them physiologically, that would really be interesting."

In earlier chapters, I examined the many ways that we have transformed youth sports, reengineering swim meets and lacrosse games to suit our grownup tastes and aspirations. Is this extreme makeover making us happy? The evidence is pretty clear. It isn't. While watching our kids play sports, we're anxious and irritable. As Goldstein's research indicates, we're angry. Behavior at youth sports events is worse than it has ever been. Not that we've ever been especially well behaved.

True, more children than ever are playing youth sports. The National Council of Youth Sports estimates that about 41 million girls and boys play on organized teams, a number that has steadily increased the past twenty years. In soccer, a sport with a historically sharp growth curve, participation among players six years of age and older shot up from 15.3 million in 1987 to more than 18 million in 1998 (before dipping in the last decade, a trend I will address a bit later), according to the Sporting Goods Manufacturers Association. (In Pop Warner Football, participation has doubled in the last fifteen years to 260,000 players, according to league statistics.)

Yet, as the population of youth players shoots up, the fun is slipping away. That's what kids tell us when we ask, which is not often enough. In 2006, the Minnesota Youth Soccer Association asked players what they had observed about their parents, coaches, and adults generally at their sports games. This is part of what they shared: 34 percent said they had been yelled at or teased by a fan, and 15 percent reported that their parents get angry when they play poorly. *Sports Illustrated for Kids* asked similar questions in a survey of its young readers. The feedback was even more disturbing: 74 percent of children said they had witnessed out-of-control adults at their games. The most common bad behavior cited: parents yelling at officials, and coaches and parents yelling at children.

Overly invested parents have become a part of the game to be overcome, like zone defenses and shoelaces that won't stay tied. "One or two parents from every team want to coach their kids. They're always trying to tell them, 'Hey, keep your eye on the ball.' Parents should be cheerleaders for their son or daughter. Coaches should be in control," says Michael Lerner, a baseball coach at Hammond High School in Columbia, Maryland.

Allison Peterson, who coached her daughter's youth soccer team in Pomfret, Connecticut, told me a memorable story. A coach for many years, she explained that when she started out she had been unprepared for one of her biggest challenges: counseling eight-year-olds on how to stay focused as their parents yelled instructions and criticisms from the sidelines. "It was often difficult for them to concentrate on the game. The girls frequently verbalized that to me," Peterson says. Peterson and her fellow coaches eventually hit on one strategy that allowed the children to cope with such distractions: inserting players with the noisiest parents into the game on the side of the field opposite where their parents were watching.

Joey Fuller, a youth soccer coach in Burke, Virginia, shared a similar experience about his daughters, ages seven and nine. He had volunteered to help supervise their teams in an athletic club in a Washington, D.C., suburb, one that he said attracted parents mostly content to leave the coaching to the coaches. There were overwrought parents, though. He recalled a situation in which a child dribbling downfield heard her parents screaming from the sidelines. With players, coaches, and other parents watching, "she stopped midgame, turned around, and made a face. She was clearly upset," says Fuller. He has witnessed similar situations that attracted less attention.

"At halftime, I saw a girl actually ask her parents to please stop yelling because she plays much better when they don't yell," Fuller says. "If you're a kid, why would you want these adults on the sidelines screaming and yelling at you?"

It's a strange role reversal that must be as awkward for children as for the adults they are preaching to. Yet, increasingly, kids are compelled to speak out. In Mahwah, New Jersey, twelve-year-old teammates Kiersten Spencer and Kirsten Stuart decided that the adults attending their games, ostensibly to root them on, were, in fact, driving them nuts. Their behavior was atrocious. Several had resorted to all manner of poor sportsmanship to unnerve players on visiting teams. Fed up, Spencer and Stuart penned an article that ran on the op-ed page of their local daily newspaper, the *Record*.

In the letter, the girls stated their case for adult restraint and self-reflection as well as any researcher or sportswriter could. "Parents are a major problem. They think winning is everything. Once when we played a basketball game... a player from the other team took a foul shot.... One of the parents 'accidentally' sneezed right before the player shot, to blow off her confidence as well as her focus. How could he do that to a twelve-year-old girl?"

Rude and rowdy is troubling enough. Youth sports have become a backdrop for behavior that's truly dangerous. To wit, two overlooked news stories from the spring of 2007: In

East Pennsboro Township, Pennsylvania, police arrested a man and charged him with harassment of his eleven-year-old son. Police said the man became angry when his son cried during a wrestling practice. As father and son sat outside a Wal-Mart in their car after the workout, police said the man struck his son in the face and punched him in the chest. Later, he ordered the boy to get out and run laps around the car.

In Lincoln, Nebraska, a mother and her fifteen-year-old daughter argued heatedly as they rode home from a soccer game. The mother was upset with her daughter's performance in the game and with her attitude after the game, police said. As they approached the Lincoln exit of Interstate 80, the mother pulled over to the shoulder and demanded that her daughter get out of the car, then drove away. A teammate's parent spotted the girl and picked her up.

These incidents are frightening. How could a dad punch his son or a mom leave her daughter on an overpass? What they are not is isolated. Such behavior occurs with distressing frequency in all corners of the country, hundreds if not thousands of them each year. The perpetrators often aren't members of some lunatic fringe, either. They're a lot like you and me. In fact, they're uncomfortably like you and me. Here are three more stories from 2007 that I include to underscore the point that youth sports has a scary power to cloud our judgment.

In Clearwater, Florida, a high school principal was accused of harassing the school's baseball coaches after they benched his son, who was batting .077 and had struck out seven times in fifteen at-bats. Citing pressure from out-of-control parents, several of the coaches resigned and one filed a complaint against the principal with the school district's office of professional standards, saying of his former boss, "I don't want him to be fired. I just want him to know what he did was wrong." The principal denied the charges.

In New Jersey, the state supreme court handed out the harshest penalty in its history against one of its own jurists, censuring Justice Roberto A. Rivera-Soto for improperly using his influence to settle a score between his sons, members of a high school football team, and the captain of the squad. The judge's twin sons, sophomores at Haddonfield Memorial High School, were involved in several arguments with the team captain and claimed that they'd been struck by an older teammate. Rivera-Soto filed a juvenile delinquency complaint for assault, and then, according to the *New York Times,* he improperly intervened in the case by contacting two judges and requesting that a prosecutor review the case. "For my actions, and the effect they may have had, I am profoundly sorry," Rivera-Soto wrote after the wrist slap.

In Santa Fe, New Mexico, Daniel Foley, Republican minority whip of the New Mexico House of Representatives, faced charges of disorderly conduct, resisting arrest, and obstructing an officer after a melee at a high school basketball game. Police said the trouble began when two basketball players began fighting and the opposing team coaches stepped in to separate them. Foley's fourteen-year-old son attempted to join in, and one coach extended his arm to restrain him. At that point, the older Foley ran onto the court, screaming profanities and spitting chewing tobacco, police said. He had to be restrained by police. (The incident clinched the politician's reputation for questionable judgment. Earlier he'd requested a flyover of F-16s for the opening of a Toyota dealership owned by a political supporter.)

Not only is such behavior spectacularly ill-advised; it also has real consequences. The tension that pervades youth sports hasn't exactly been a boon for recruitment of youth sports officials. Already low-paying, the positions become less attractive as coaches and parents drive up the pressure. In many states, a shortage of officials has become a serious and chronic problem. The National Federation of State High School Associations reported a nearly 20 percent drop in officials from 2002 to 2006. In Wyoming, a skeleton crew of sixteen officials covered the state's entire high school football schedule several years ago. The reality is that there are less stressful ways to make a buck. "People just don't want the hassles anymore," a Texas school official told the *New Orleans Times-Picayune.*

Many states have laws specifically addressing violence against sports officials. In 2007, twenty-three states had carved out special penalties for assaulting a referee or an umpire. In California, assaulting a sports official is punishable by a $2,000 fine and up to a year-long sentence in the county jail. It's more than a theoretical problem. According to researchers David Rainey of John Carroll University and Peter Duggan of Ball State, slightly more than 10 percent of officials included in two major studies reported that they had been assaulted at some point in their careers. The majority of these assaults were carried out by adults, often parents and coaches. On its Web site, the National Association of Sports Officials (NASO) lists more than a hundred attacks, including one after a baseball game for seven-year-olds. In that case, a Louisiana man followed an umpire into the restroom, shoved him, and threatened to kill him. He was upset that the two coaches of his son's team were ejected from the game for disputing the umpire's calls.

Sports officials can always sign up for assault protection insurance. The National Association of Sports Officials offers this benefit, which kicks in when an official is "the victim of an assault and/or battery by a spectator, fan, or participant." Benefits include $100 for each game the victim misses because of injury and a free legal consultation for those who want to pursue lawsuits against their attackers. "We're providing a tremendous service to our members," NASO president Barry Mano explains. For the most part, violence spurred by youth sports attracts relatively little attention until the consequences are so jolting that we cannot ignore them. In 2000, Thomas Junta, forty-two, arrived at an indoor hockey rink in suburban Boston to pick up his son and another young boy who'd been skating. Before he left, he'd all but killed a man. Eventually, Michael Costin died from the pummeling he took at the hands of Junta, a fight that was kindled by some rough hockey involving their sons. Junta was convicted of manslaughter and sentenced to six years in prison. "The sad thing is you have one family with no father and another family with a father in jail," Martha Coakley, the prosecutor in the case, told me. "It wasn't an inevitable result."

What lessons do such incidents teach our children? Not that the umpire is always right, of course. And absolutely nothing about the elements of good sportsmanship. Instead, the message is that anything goes—at least until the police arrive to break things up.

It's worse than we think, if we believe the findings of the Los Angeles–based Josephson Institute. In 2007, the non-profit research institute went public with results of a survey on ethics and high school sports. Over two years, the institute's researchers canvassed 5,275 high school athletes, asking them to consider the ethical lines they would cross to win a big game or meet. For some the answer was almost any line.

From the Josephson Institute study:

A basketball coach teaches young players to illegally hold and push in ways that are difficult to detect. Proper: 47 percent of male basketball players.

In baseball, the coach instructs the groundskeeper to build up the third base line slightly to help keep bunts fair. Proper: 36 percent of baseball players.

A player trash-talks his defender after every score, demeaning the defender's skills. Proper: 42 percent of male athletes.

To get his team worked up, the coach deliberately swears at an official to get thrown out of the game. Proper: 40 percent of baseball players.

The Josephson study reports that girls have a "deeper commitment to honesty and fair play" than boys. Actually, much deeper.

Girls were about half as likely as boys to "boo, taunt,

and jeer opponents" from the bench and, far more than their male classmates, tended to frown on unsportsmanlike acts, from surreptitiously reviewing a rival team's scouting report to tricking a referee or umpire into ejecting the opponent's star player in response to a foul that never occurred.

Most startling is what the survey suggests about high school athletes, male and female, away from the gym or track: In school, they're more likely to cheat than classmates who don't play sports. Of those on sports teams, 65 percent said they'd cheated at least once in the past year, compared to 60 percent for nonathletes, statistics that hardly cover either group in glory. Among the athletes, the most prolific cheaters were football players (72 percent) and cheerleaders (71 percent)!

Josephson researchers offer several theories for this enhanced propensity to cheat. For instance, athletes could be reacting to the pressures to stay eligible to compete on their sports team or to difficulties managing their time. Not mentioned are lessons that might have been picked up in the heat of a peewee hockey game. By the time they reach high school, teen athletes have had almost a dozen years of exposure to moms, dads, and volunteer coaches whose attitudes about playing by the rules, and breaking them, they've closely observed. What have we taught them?

If there is an iconic youth sports spectacle to rival the Little League World Series, it is the Soap Box Derby. Started in 1934 in Dayton, Ohio, the derby is the only kids sporting event in the world that you can't win without a big toolbox. There's more involved, obviously. The young champions also need to be carpenters, engineers, mechanics, and, on race day, dandy drivers.

Gravity makes the race. The cars are not engine-driven. In Akron, where the race moved in 1936, they zip down a steep straightaway at speeds up to thirty-five miles per hour on standardized wheels with precision ball bearings. During the glory days of the race in the 1950s and 1960s, as many as seventy thousand fans showed up to watch the cars glide to the finish and to toast the winning drivers, boys and girls, for cracking the code of aerodynamics.

That's the way the Soap Box Derby is supposed to go. But over the years, the race's reputation has taken an awful beating. Lots of people are responsible for the troubles that have befallen it and, not surprising, almost all are adults. The worst of the derby's setbacks have been caused by cheating scandals. And the most notorious cheater in the race's history is Robert Lange Sr.

In 1973, Lange's nephew and ward, fourteen-year-old Jimmy Gronen, won the Soap Box Derby. Gronen's derby car handled like a dream. It was such a dream, in fact, that the families of the other 138 racers became suspicious. They demanded that race officials examine the car to prove to them that it had been put together according to the strict derby rules. The inspection of Gronen's car led to a shocking discovery. Officials found a hidden button and a wire, and, tucked away in the nose, a magnet. As Melanie Payne describes in *Champions, Cheaters, and Childhood Dreams: Memories of the Soap Box Derby,* Gronen, with help from Lange, had rigged up the car so that it drove more like a Maserati.

As recounted by Payne, "After Gronen was at the gate, he would lean his helmet back and flip on a switch that sent a current from the battery in the back of the car to the magnet in the nose. Thus engaged, the magnet would pull the car forward as the metal flap dropped, propelling the car out of the starting position and down the ramp."

The derby held a news conference to expose the fraud. In front of reporters, Gronen's car was literally sawed in half, laying bear the wires and the entire conspiracy. Lange later owned up to the scam, but the spectacle wounded the race dearly. One of the prosecutors who probed the Gronen case sighed and said, "It's like seeing apple pie, motherhood, and the American flag grinding to a halt."

That cheating scandal is a footnote compared to the most

notorious name in the history of youth sports ethics: Danny Almonte. It's too bad about that, because Danny was, more or less, an innocent in the ruse of ruses that bears his name.

Go back to 2001 and the Little League World Series. The best pitcher that summer, maybe in the history of Little League, was a gangly, rangy, fireball of a player named Danny Almonte. He was just twelve years old at the time, or so everyone thought. He was close to unhittable in Williamsport, striking out batter after batter and boosting his team from the Bronx to a fine third-place finish. It was an unimaginable thrill for the boy and his father, Felipe, both immigrants from the Dominican Republic.

For a few days, Danny was the most talked-about baseball player in America, Little League, big league, or any league. The chatter wasn't all about his fastball, though. Rumors swirled that Almonte wasn't actually twelve and that his father had slipped him into Little League with a doctored birth certificate. Investigations followed, including one by *Sports Illustrated,* which dispatched two reporters to a civil records building in Almonte's hometown in the Dominican Republic. Dominican officials finally confirmed that Almonte was, in fact, fourteen years old. No wonder he had been that good.

Little League Baseball banned Felipe Almonte for life for the shenanigans, along with the president of the tainted Bronx Little League. Prosecutors in the Dominican Republic filed criminal charges against Felipe Almonte for having falsified a birth certificate. Danny didn't know anything about the scam, in part because he didn't speak English at the time. He was cleared by Little League Baseball.

As noted in chapter one, there's abundant evidence that parents have long had difficulty separating themselves emotionally and otherwise from the sports activities of their children. The impact may be greater in the age of ESPN and Tiger Woods. But the struggle is not new.

In 1953, police were called to an unremarkable house on an unremarkable street in Elgin, Illinois, a Chicago suburb.

When they arrived, they found twelve-year-old Gary Molner on the porch chained to a chair. One end of the twelve-foot chain was looped around his neck; the other passed through the arm of a metal chair and was fastened with a padlock. A photograph of the downcast boy, shackles dangling from his neck, appeared in the *Chicago Daily Tribune*. Molner told police that his father was punishing him for playing with matches, failing to do yard work, and because he was "dissatisfied with the son's performance in a Little League baseball game Sunday."

Then there was the celebrated case of Louis J. Castellano Jr., perhaps the only Little League coach to ask the supreme court of New York to save his job. Castellano, a man who loved kids and loved to win, coached in the Hempstead, Long Island, Little League. In 1969, after a tough opening day loss, Castellano had a brief confrontation with the mother of a player, the team's pitching star, about the boy's failure to show up for the game. The exchange became so heated that the boy's mother contacted the Little League's board of director, demanding that Castellano be fired. The league obliged, canning him at midseason. Much maneuvering followed, culminating with Castellano's appeal to the supreme court of New York, which needed a mere two weeks to dismiss the ludicrous case.

These frightful stories establish that our generation did not invent youth sports dysfunction. We may have polished it, perfected it, yes, taken it to new levels of absurdity. We didn't invent it. Similarly, it helps explode one of the most durable myths about youth sports: that there was an idyllic, Norman Rockwell era when children played purely for fun and parents gathered happily on the sidelines with absolutely no interest in the final score. If such a period ever occurred, my guess is that it lasted forty-eight hours. Maybe, just maybe, our generation can help change course.

9   A RETURN TO FUNDAMENTALS

During a typical summer in Fort Wayne, Indiana, children sign up to play in an assortment of the usual organized sports leagues—and one that is unusual. It's called the Wildcat Baseball League, and its guiding principle is that sports for children are recreational and not a career. Dale McMillen, a local businessman and philanthropist, founded the league in 1961, according to legend, after watching a group of children glumly slink off after being told they'd missed the cut at a baseball tryout. He resolved to form a league that would spare young players the same disappointment. He chose a fitting motto: "Everybody makes the team." In 2007, 2,984 youth players made the team in Wildcat Baseball's various divisions, ranging from Kitten (6-7) to Tiger (13-14). They played on athletic fields in and around Fort Wayne from June until August. For the most part, it was baseball the way it's played on youth diamonds everywhere. Yet there are some distinctive characteristics about Wildcat Baseball. The league plays ball only during daylight, with different teams taking the field every ninety minutes or so, from eight a.m. to three p.m. So players never miss dinner at home because of a baseball game. The Wildcat coaches are high school and college students selected by the league and paid salaries.

Their duties are different from typical youth coaches. Rather than being assigned one team, they work with many teams and dozens of young players in a season. During a game, one coach might help out with both teams while the second serves as the umpire. Parents aren't asked—or permitted—to be coaches. They can attend the games as spectators.

Winning matters but so does learning the fundamentals. During a Wildcat game, it is common for play to stop while a coach gives a brief lesson about, say, how to stick out a fielder's mitt.

When the season ends, it really ends. There are no all-star games or travel teams. The talented players aren't celebrated more than ones who went the whole season without a hit. The only trophies for personal accomplishments go to players who rack up perfect attendance. There is no postseason banquet, and there aren't even team photos to buy. Offering these perks "would put us right back in the Little League mentality," says Bill Derbyshire, president of Wildcat Baseball. "Our philosophy is that we're not going to continually be handing out stuff to the players."

In theory and in practice, Wildcat Baseball is an idea that works. In nearly five decades, the program has graduated 175,000 youth players, including some who went on to become doctors, lawyers, and in one case, a soap opera star. By all accounts, most look back on playing as a formative experience that always put fun first.

Ansel Sanders and Nick D'Ambrosio run a summer sports camp that's far from ordinary. That much is obvious from the name that the public school teachers and coaches picked for their creation: Athletes and Authors. Sanders and Mr. D, as campers call him, host Athletes and Authors four weeks during the summer out of a public elementary and middle school building in Baltimore, charging a modest $200 a week (with a discount of $720 for families who sign up for the entire month). Kids show up in their shorts and T-shirts every day knowing they're going to be playing sports with their friends, anything from soccer and flag football to lacrosse and basketball. Before the day is over, they'll also be exercising their brains.

The camp directors use the kids' fascination with sports to sneak in a daily lesson in language arts. One seventy-five-minute period is set aside each day for campers to read books about sports, discuss newspaper and magazine articles on current events in sports, and research sports topics on the Internet. The curriculum varies from session to session, depending on what's in the news and what moves the campers. Recent groups have read *Let Them Play* by Margot Theis Raven, "Amigo Brothers" by Piri Thomas, and *Profiles in Sports Courage* by Ken Rappaport. More inspiration comes from guest speakers who are, not surprisingly, athletes and authors.

Sanders and D'Ambrosio are worthy mentors. D'Ambrosio is a physical education teacher and lacrosse coach in the Baltimore public schools. Sanders's résumé almost glows. A former lacrosse all-American at Washington and Lee University, the unrelentingly upbeat camp founder earned a master's in teaching from Johns Hopkins and taught eighth-grade language arts in public schools for many years, in addition to coaching elementary school soccer and lacrosse teams to several city championships. The concept they've dreamt up is working. Camp enrollment doubled in two years, and the directors have new ideas about using sports to teach life lessons.

In a poor section of Marietta, Georgia, kids spill onto the streets and head for a row of old tennis courts next to a couple of weathered apartment buildings. They're young and impressionable—eight to twelve years old. They might be headed for trouble if it weren't for the soccer league that suddenly has sprouted up in their hard-scrabble community. Atlanta-based Soccer in the Streets teamed up with the local police athletic league to make this program happen. The nonprofit supplied soccer balls and goals, coached the volunteer coaches, and, as it has in seventy-five American cities, provided the inspiration.

Jill Robbins and her husband, Harvey, are the driving forces behind Soccer in the Streets. Jill is executive director, a tireless advocate, and fundraiser. Harvey is the teacher and coach. They seek out partnerships with schools and rec centers in low-income communities and then contribute the infrastructure needed to get a soccer program off the ground. The partners supply the kids. For inner-city schools with no budget for sports programs, this is a remarkably good deal. Often, these schools are struggling to engage children from troubled backgrounds, kids who don't show up regularly for classes and behave badly when they do. Soccer in the Streets has been effective in reaching such at-risk students. During an eighteen-week program at one school, peer conflict among young players decreased 81 percent, from three in five players to one in eight. The program also helped students, often fourth and fifth graders, to learn to relate to adults, reducing incidents of students arguing, becoming belligerent, and "rolling their eyes in frustration" by 75 percent.

Over time, some of the students become enthusiastic, even competent soccer players. But that's hardly the point. "A lot of these kids have the weight of the world on their shoulders. They are interpreters for their parents and baby-sitters for their siblings. They don't know what, if anything, they'll have for dinner that night. For us to let them come out and be kids for a change, to not worry about who is going to get an advantage over them, that's worth a lot," says Jill Robbins.

These youth sports programs are all very different from each other, of course. Wildcat Baseball is a summer program for kids in the Midwest who want to play baseball for fun and don't expect to be on a fast train to the major leagues. If Athletes and Authors has a goal, it's to bridge the gap between the sports that young kids love and the academic pursuits they're not sure about yet. Soccer in the Streets is a lifeline to kids seeking refuge from the harsh world beyond the goalposts.

What unites these successful programs, though, is that

they are designed for kids, about kids, and with the best interests of kids in mind. The same cannot be said of many youth sports programs across the country. It may have been true at one time in the distant past. Now too many programs are tailored for the big people who stand on the sidelines. They must be because they are extremely ill-suited to the emotional needs and physical needs of the young players. This is not a revelation for which I can claim full credit. Thinking about the issue, I am reminded of a conversation several years ago with William Pollack, author of *Real Boys* and a child psychologist at Harvard Medical School. The subject was the Little League World Series. I had asked the psychologist whether the world series was still the wholesome, kid-centered event that Little League officials insist it is. The images that most TV watchers took away year after year is happy players jumping up and down, having more fun than twelve-year-olds dreamed of. It didn't look like torture. Yet when I pose a question to the good doctor, he bristles. "I can't believe what we've created is for kids. It started out for kids, but it's becoming a training ground for professional activity," he says. "It's like putting a little boy in a man's suit."

Millions of young athletes are walking around in those adult uniforms, loose around the hips. What can be done to address the problem and give their games back to them? Heeding the words of Dr. Pollack is a starting point. Let's remember the consumers of youth sports. They ought not to be TV networks, sporting goods manufacturers, or travel tour operators. They shouldn't be adults. They are girls and boys ages three to seventeen. All our decisions as parents, coaches, league presidents, and food-stand operators should be made with their welfare in mind. In a better world, our dreams and aspirations would not count.

For decades, we've been warned that the hostile takeover of youth sports by grownups has changed youth sports for the worst: by the NEA in 1952, the AMA in 1958, and by Carl Stotz for the last four decades of his life. In 1976, Thomas

Tutko, considered by many the father of sports psychology, wrote, "We organize children's leagues, give them uniforms, hand out trophies, set up playoffs and All-Star teams, send them to 'bowl' games, and encourage them to compete at earlier and earlier ages. In the eyes of many parents and coaches, it's apparently never too early to get a jump on the family next door, the pros or the Russians."

Despite these siren calls, there was no reform movement, or none that left even a modest impression. Youth sports marched on without a missed step. Before the games can change, we will have to. We can move toward that goal if we take a few modest steps.

One is to listen to doctors. Sports medicine doctors are offering plenty of advice about the risks our children run when they play the same sport year-round or don't give their bodies time to recover between seasons. For the most part, we're ignoring them. Overuse injuries now account for as much as 50 percent of all medical issues related to sports play. And think about it: Every one of the hundreds of thousands of those sore shoulders and tender wrists is preventable, sports doctors say.

Lyle Micheli, the renowned pediatric sports medicine physician, considers coach education key to addressing overuse injuries. Micheli believes education classes should be required before leagues issue coaches their clipboards. He even advocates a certification program, with coaches going to class, passing a test, and getting some sort of patch to wear on their sleeve to show they've completed the course. He says the important material could be covered in fifteen to sixteen hours and the course taken online. "People say it's crazy. It's hard enough as it is getting volunteer coaches," Micheli says, brushing off such naysayers. "In Canada, Australia, and New Zealand, they've done it. They found they get more coaches."

Voluntary training would be easier to arrange and monitor for youth leagues. But the programs must be mandatory for two reasons, Micheli believes. First, the ad hoc information campaign that doctors have been leading for years isn't reaching enough parents and likely never will. One problem is the rapid turnover of adults involved in youth sports. There is little to no institutional memory in most youth leagues. As children grow up and out of sports programs, so do their parents. The information they have absorbed is gone. "I'll go to Newton [Massachusetts] and speak to Little League coaches," says Micheli. "Number one, only the good coaches show up. Number two, every six or seven years, it's a totally different group. We're starting from scratch again–'Little League elbow, what's that?'"

Second, Micheli says, waves of new volunteer coaches have to be continually alerted to the fact that more training for children does not always equal improved performance. In the patients he treats by the dozens, the opposite often is true. "A volunteer swimming coach may not know anything about the science of swimming, but he can always tell little Mary Lou, 'You swam four thousand yards yesterday. Let's do four thousand five hundred yards today,'" says Micheli. "The message is, if you want to succeed, work harder. It's wrong."

The experts training elite youth athletes acknowledge they have more to learn. In November 2007, the International Olympic Committee published a "consensus statement" voicing concern about the health effects on young athletes training for international competitions. Micheli was one of the statement's ten authors, as were Janet Evans, a former U.S. Olympic swimmer; a Swiss psychologist; and an Argentine cardiologist. That the august IOC would acknowledge youth athletes are being harmed by excessive and reckless training is news itself. Significantly, the panel reported that even at the elite level, "more research [should] be done to better identify the parameters of training the elite athlete, which must be communicated effectively to the coach, athlete parents, sport governing bodies and the scientific community."

Discouraging early specialization is also a key, says John

DiFiori. In his practice, DiFiori meets parents who've bought into the conventional wisdom that the way to raise a champion is to narrow a child's focus to a single sport sooner rather than later. Despite the specter of a two-year-old Tiger Woods whacking golf balls on *The Mike Douglas Show,* DiFiori doubts that. The problem is, he can't prove it.

"The concept that you must be participating at a certain level at a certain age to guarantee that success, there's no data to show that's true and it might be quite the contrary," DiFiori says. "I tell parents, 'Expose your children to a variety of sports, as well as other activities: music, [other] outdoor activities. Sooner or later, they'll pick up something that they're enthusiastic about and probably be successful at.' That seems preferable to me to choosing a sport because someone said your child looks like a lacrosse player. That's the Soviet, eastern bloc model."

"These parents are not bad people. They mean well. They absolutely mean well. There is just too much emphasis on winning and not on developing players or having a good time," says Dr. Joseph Chandler. Chandler is referring to the youth baseball scene in his hometown of Atlanta. Chandler is as passionate as any doctor I have spoken with about the abuse of young pitchers from chronic overuse. He's not a finger pointer at either parents or coaches. He is a believer that strong measures must be taken to protect talented young players. He'd ban curveballs for children under fourteen. And if Chandler were youth sports czar there would be no more twelve-month baseball seasons for youth players. "I would strike a match and burn travel teams. Without travel teams, you will not have year-round baseball," he says.

Most troubling to Chandler is that coaches are in denial. They fail to recognize the part they played in an injury that occurs three, five, six years after a child has been on their team. Notes Chandler, "Often their story is 'I know I am teaching right. Because I've been coaching Little League for ten years and I've never had a kid injured.' They don't think they've done anything wrong. We need to get the message out that it's not during your watch that we expect these injuries. The effect is cumulative, so they occur later, at eighteen, nineteen, twenty years old."

"Changing behavior, that doesn't happen in one day," says Eric Small, one of the nation's top sports medicine doctors for children. He isn't predicting an epiphany any time soon. A minority of the adults who bring their children to his office in Mount Kisco, New York, for the most part aren't seeking higher truths about overuse injuries. They want their children better and back on the field or the ice. "For the most part, [the parents] think their child is so talented or they're trying to keep up with the Joneses...even though they're doing more harm than good," says Small.

Listening to children is another way to heal youth sports. Michael Stuart, a Mayo Clinic orthopedic surgeon and chief medical officer for USA Hockey, has three sons who have played professional hockey and a daughter who starred on Boston College's varsity hockey team. The sport was as much a part of the Stuart family routine as breathing. Yet before the start of each hockey season, Stuart says, "I always made a point of asking each of my children a very important question: 'Do you want to play hockey this year?' The response is always, 'Of course, Dad! This is what I was looking forward to.' I didn't ask the question because I didn't know the answer, I asked so my children would know there was no expectation. It was their choice. The point was made to them. 'Gee, I don't really have to play. Dad is even asking me if I want to.' The bottom line for children, or anyone, playing sports is you have to enjoy it. It's hard to reach your potential if you're miserable."

In my reporting, I met a number of young adults whose insights into youth sports—its assets and excesses—were impressive. One was Katy Justice, now a college student and aspiring journalist at the University of Texas. When I met Katy she was an infant. Her parents, Richard and Marty, are longtime friends. Richard is a popular sports columnist at the *Houston Chronicle*. Marty is a sports mom who lived in an intense sports world without allowing her children to be consumed by it.

Katy and her sister, Lizzie, have been competitive swimmers nearly all their lives. Katy started at age four and swam until her senior year of high school, when she stopped with the support of her parents. Most of those years, Katy was swimming with one of the most competitive teams in the country, the Woodlands Swim Team, aka TWST.

Marty explained to me just how competitive: "We do know people that use [asthma] inhalers to get their kids hyped before every race, growth enhancers to build muscle, concoctions that they actually mix up in their own kitchens that are meant to 'replace' minerals depleted from their muscles. They see outside coaches beyond their own coaches to perfect their strokes, and they start that when they are little and continue it until the kids get so sick of it, they walk out one day. Strangely, the largest percent of the kids that are good enough to get scholarships on to college don't continue to swim past their second year. The hours it demands, plus the grades they have to maintain, winds up being way too much for them to handle."

The time that Katy put into swimming was startling. At the point she stopped swimming, her Woodlands team was practicing six days a week, four hours each day. Every school day began with a workout. Mondays, Wednesdays, and Fridays, the day began with swim practice at five thirty a.m. that lasted two hours or longer. After school, it was back to the pool at three for another session ending after five. Tuesday and Thursday mornings were a break of sorts. Instead of pool training on those days, Katy and her teammates did distance running starting at six a.m.

"We had a three-story high school. I dreaded those days that I'd have to go to the third floor. My legs were so tired," Katy told me. "When I quit swimming, the feeling was amazing. The first two periods of class, I wasn't falling asleep."

The decision to quit was Katy's to make. Her parents

supported her swimming with time, encouragement, and money—thousands of dollars each year in everything from swimsuits to overnight trips to meets. They made those commitments for her enjoyment and benefit, not the other way around. "We have always told our kids that the day it's not fun anymore...all they have to do is say so. Katy literally called me after school one day and said she wanted to quit that day. And I told her to go tell the coaches. I wasn't even there. And she did and it was over," says her mom.

Katy hasn't cut her ties with competitive swimming. She still spends time at the pool rooting for her sister, Lizzie. But she left swimming on the best of terms. "People ask me all the time, do I miss it? Not at all."

"It's easy to become obsessed with things, especially if you don't have the right dream," says Francis Murray, who was convinced he wanted to be a Division I college athlete, until he became one. "I had a dream that was a bit out there. Unfortunately, I lost some time."

Although he doesn't blame anyone for his hasty decisions, Murray reflects on his high school years and wonders whether he could have chosen his mentors more carefully. "In my high school, athletics was so pumped up. It not only was important, it trumped academics completely. The kids who were good at sports, whose names got in the newspaper, they were popular and got the girls. It was the [focus] of a lot of the teachers and coaches, too. They put a whole lot of emphasis on [college sports] because they had gone down that road and played Division I."

There may not be any global solutions to the challenges facing youth sports, but in communities in all corners of the country, concerned adults are organizing. They're seeking to restore a sense of perspective to kids' games and, in some cases, to mute the impact of overly invested adults. In Duval County, Florida, parents, players, and coaches are required to sign a sportsmanship "contract" before the season begins. In Naples, Florida, calling out to a player during a game can cost a parent $45. In Minnesota, a parents' coalition known as Balance4Success declared a moratorium on youth sports practices, games, and tournaments on Sundays. Parents who join the movement affirm a Take Back Sundays pledge that, in part, reads, "I do not want my child to be overscheduled; even high school and collegiate varsity athletes traditionally take Sundays off from practices and games; and I know that cultural change towards more balanced living requires a unified stand by many parents."

A few thousand miles away in Louisiana, the Baton Rouge Soccer Association is experimenting with Silent Weekends, a program that has had modest success in a handful of youth leagues around the country. The concept is simple and, when it works, reduces noise at youth sports events to the yelps of players and chirping crickets. Some leagues put limits on what parents and coaches can say. In others, they can't speak at all.

In 1999, a girls youth soccer league in an affluent suburb of Cleveland started the movement to end adult chatter. Parents weren't at all pleased with the first Silent Saturday. "For the first couple of years, we had parents all over us. They were saying we were Hitler, we were dictators, we were violating their First Amendment rights," an Ohio girls soccer league official told the *New York Times*. The idea has since been copied and modified by dozens of leagues. For example, the Central Pennsylvania Youth Soccer League forces parents and coaches into silence by distributing a truckload of lollipops. In 2007, it passed out thirty thousand suckers during Silent Soccer weekend.

In Baton Rouge, the noise reduction protocol is a bit more complicated. Cheering for players on both teams not only is permitted but encouraged, says Gary Buete, executive director of the soccer league. Adults may not engage in sideline coaching, meaning yell any sort of instruction to the young players. "The game is for the kids. Ideally, we let them play and they learn by making their own decisions. Instead, what happened was parents and coaches constantly were shouting instructions. Players never learned to make decisions on their own," says Buete.

The first time the Baton Rouge program used the new rule it was a qualified success. If anything, the sidelines became too quiet—"an eerie atmosphere of dead silence," according to Buete. "Our instructions [to the parents and coaches] were: Cheer, scream, yell, shout encouragement. But what we got was very little encouragement. One, parents weren't sure what they *couldn't* say. Two, they didn't know *how* to cheer without shouting instructions."

After the first season of Silent Weekend, Buete surveyed coaches, players, and parents about the program. As he recalls, parents were split and coaches were mostly opposed. That left the youth players. "They loved it," he says.

The lesson is straightforward enough. Children mostly want to be left alone to pursue their interests in their ways. That's a bruising message for adults, but I maintain a hard truth. Where is the evidence? The Sporting Goods Manufacturers Association, a respected trade organization that tracks sports participation trends in America, reports two particularly interesting ones. In the sports in which adults are coaches, organizers, and vocal fans, the SGMA reports a clear slump. From 1998 to 2004, participation slid in soccer (13 percent), baseball (21 percent), and ice hockey (30 percent). The percentages moved in the opposite direction for so-called action sports, edgy, high-energy, largely unsupervised activities in which kids generally are free to make—and break—their own rules. Over the same six years, numbers of snowboarders climbed 30 percent and skateboarders soared 47 percent. To be fair, these numbers hardly spell the demise of adult-run sports leagues. Even with the drop in play, soccer still attracted nearly 16 million players in 2004, more than double the number of Americans who discovered the joys of snowboarding. Basketball players are a nation unto themselves—34 million. The study's methodology also leaves room for interpretation. For instance, a participant is anyone playing a sport at least once a year. A basketball player shooting hoops four days a week counts as one, same as a skateboarder who headed for the skate park one morning all year. Still, there is a powerful message in the success of action sports and it might be this: Kids can have fun without us, even more fun.

Paul Rodriguez Jr. helped me understand how completely different it is to be a kid obsessed with an action sport than one who plays travel team soccer. I met Rodriguez at the X Games in Los Angeles. A slight, wiry guy with an easy smile, he is a professional skateboarder. He was twenty-two at the time, and already a multimillionaire from prize winnings and a slew of endorsement deals, including an especially lucrative one with Nike. Rodriquez's father, Paul Sr., is a well-known TV director and standup comic. Rodriguez told me his parents were indifferent when he became interested in his sport at age twelve. "I wouldn't say they were gung ho about skateboarding, but they weren't anti-skateboarding," he says. They bought him his board and shoes and wished him good luck. His mother allowed him to hang out at the skate park, he says, "as long as my grades were somewhat decent." At eighteen, he decided to become a professional skateboarder. For his parents, there was none of the pride that comes with a child who becomes a star football player or a big league baseball player. "When I told my dad this was going to be my career, he said, 'Son, are you kidding me? Do you really think you can make any money doing *that?*' They were normal parental worries. I don't blame him," Rodriguez told me. "My dad is a comedian. He had to do the exact same thing with his family. I guess it just runs in the genes." For several years, Paul Sr. stayed away from his son's competitions, declining his invitations to attend the X Games, the world series of action sports. Now he's a big fan. Go to Paul Sr.'s show business Web site and you find a link to his son's pro skateboarding Web site. Says the son, "He's now very supportive of the fact that I found something I love."

There's an irony, of course. The more we embrace our children's sports, the more we impose ourselves into their private world. The more we do that, by definition, the less our children's sports belong to them, which explains their appeal in the first place. It's happening in action sports. The first generation of action sports kiddies has reached parenthood. They understand skateboarding and motocross biking and feel connected to them in the way 1980s parents did to basketball and softball. Already, the action sports world has been yanked into the mainstream. Tony Hawk, the skateboarding legend, sells his signature line of slacks and polo shirts at Kohl's. The X Games, ESPN's action sports winner in the ratings, is nearly the television spectacle of the Olympics. Let's face it. We can't help ourselves.

POSTSCRIPT

Ben had his sutures removed in January. Before we left for the orthopedic office, he asked me to bring the camera. That night, he posted on his Facebook page photos of the nurse snipping away, making it the most widely viewed doctor's visit I could remember in our family. This was the first of numerous milestones in Ben's recovery. Others quickly followed: Ben fully straightening his right elbow, tossing a baseball for the first time, playing catch again in the yard, whizzing fastballs at nearly full speed. There were setbacks, of course, spasms, aches, and concerns about whether the pains he was reporting were anything to worry about. They all faded. Eight months after surgery, Ben was thinking about playing baseball again.

Open tryouts for the George Washington University intercollegiate baseball team would be in the fall. Ben intended to be there, in the best shape of his life. He made plans to spend the entire month of August in Tempe, Arizona, at Athletes' Performance, a high-end fitness salon where football pros JaMarcus Russell and DeAngelo Hall and baseball players Chase Utley and Russell Martin, among many others, have trained. The price for his comprehensive fitness program came to $5,000, money Peggy and I agreed would have to come out of his bank account. Ben spent June and July working two jobs to earn what he needed. Then, just as he had planned, he left for Athletes' Performance, blogging about the experiences most days for the next four weeks. I soon began to wonder whether I should be in Arizona with my son. In one of his early posts, Ben wrote, "I learned yesterday that we will receive 'shooters' before every workout. For me, those shooters are about 8 oz of creatine and 8 oz of EAS Muscle Armour [another dietary supplement]. All supplements that we receive here are ethical and NCAA-approved."

Nice try, but I wasn't comforted. I called Ben and shared my concern. Was this really necessary? Ben's ambition had overtaken mine. I was uneasy with the direction we (did I say "we"?) were headed.

I traded e-mails with Andy Cosgarea on the creatine issue. He hardly was a fan of supplements. But he calmed me down, telling me that as long as Ben drank plenty of water the creatine was harmless. (One effect of creatine is to cause dehydration.) I passed on the advice to my son, feeling better but amazed at how complicated this had become. Over the next few weeks, we received plenty of updates from Ben, mostly reassuring ones about nutritional counseling, weight training, and his table tennis victories over Koren Robinson, a Green Bay Packers player who became his buddy. For Ben, the most important news was that his arm felt better and better. When he was ready to leave for home, he was in the best shape of his life. But there was a hitch. He wouldn't be cleared to resume throwing from a pitching mound until the one-year anniversary of his surgery in December, per instructions from Cosgarea. Tryouts at GW were set for October. That meant Ben would have to audition for the team at a position other than the only one at which he stood even a sliver of a chance. Ben had known that before his fitness junket to Arizona, of course. Somehow, he figured the hard work would pay off.

The tryout was a disappointment for Ben, a few ground

balls at third, a few swings at bat, and then a few weeks waiting to hear whether he'd be called back for a second look. The
call never came. He was let down, understandably, but that
was a fleeting thing. In a few weeks, Ben had hooked on with
the GW club baseball team. His baseball life was finding balance again. More serious than intramural, less competitive
than intercollegiate athletics, club sports are an overlooked
option on many college campuses. There are no athletic scholarships or year-round training at the club level. The number
of club sports varies, but on some campuses the choices are
mind-boggling. Penn State's roster of sixty-three club teams
includes cricket, Korean karate, and snowboarding.

Another important distinction between club and varsity
sports is who does the coaching. At the varsity level, coaches
are full-time professionals, paid employees whose livelihoods
depend on winning games, or at least competing well. Club
teams don't have the money for that. Nor would they fit the
do-it-yourself mentality of these play-to-win, but play-for-fun
teams. The coaches are the players themselves, with juniors
and seniors who have been involved in the activity a few
years often taking the lead.

GW's club baseball team had such a coach, a diligent
junior and part-time pitcher named Chris Murphy. With
Chris at the helm and other students helping out, the GW
team plays fall and spring schedules, all told about twenty to
twenty-five games during the school year. The players wear
spiffy gold and blue uniforms they've paid for themselves,
and they play the University of Maryland, Loyola, and Tow-
son, all within an hour's drive of campus.

In the fall of 2007, Ben attended a tryout and showed
enough to make the club team. He was under orders from
Dr. Cosgarea to hold off on pitching until the spring, but
had clearance for almost everything else. He sent an instant
message telling me the good news. The next day, I got another message inviting Peggy and me to see him play for the
first time since his surgery. There was no turning down an
offer like that. On a chilly November night, we drove down

I-95 to an impressive high school field, with bright lights and a stand of tall, metal bleachers rising behind home plate. In total, there might have been eight spectators. We sat three rows from the field, with a partial view into the GW dugout. Then, as my wife knit furiously to keep warm, I watched my son return to baseball. We stayed three innings, long enough to watch him play catcher, bat twice, and mingle with his new college buddies. There were no coaches around barking instructions. Except for the sounds of our chattering teeth, the bleachers were deadly quiet. Ben was having the time of his life.

ACKNOWLEDGMENTS

There may be people out there with no opinion about the purpose, direction, and management of youth sports today. In the year I spent working on this book, I didn't meet many of them. (Come to think of it, *any* of them.) I am grateful to all those parents, coaches, surgeons, family practice doctors, ex-big leaguers, and, of course, children who shared their experiences and opinions, even when it was not comfortable to do so. My special thanks go out to Tommy John and Frank Jobe. They contributed immeasurably to the project and, because of them, I now can spell *palmaris longus*.

When researching kids sports games dating back almost one hundred years, libraries and university archives are helpful things. I had remarkable support in that regard from Dave Kelly at the Library of Congress, Deborah Margolis and Bob Burke at Baltimore's Enoch Pratt Free Library, and the New York University archives. If anyone needs a dossier on early-twentieth-century perspectives about sports specialization, see me.

Friends and colleagues allowed me to think out loud about the ideas contained in this book for two years and offered pure encouragement. To be sure, the views expressed in these pages are mine, not theirs. Thanks to all of them, especially Loren Feldman, Peter Land, Alan Schwarz, John Eisenberg, Ken Rosenthal, Jamie Trecker, David Hyman, Bill Hyman, Doug Abrams, Gene Bratek, David Case, Charlie Malko, Bill Greenwell, Rob Slade, Jim Dale, Ken Karpay, Jeff Helman, Michael Bryant, Mike Ricigliano, Helen and Jerome Jones, and Professor Brad Snyder. Mike Ollove may have been the most saintly of all. Like no one else, Mike was a steadying influence during the critical early months of the project. Thanks to my bosses at *BusinessWeek,* Ciro Scotti and Harry Maurer, for permitting me to play extended hooky while I finished the book. Thanks to Little League parents who got it right—my mother, Evelyn, and late father, Tony.

I am grateful to Andrew Blauner, my literary agent, for ably representing me and for guiding the book to Beacon Press and to a superb editor, Helene Atwan. Allison Trzop, an assistant editor at Beacon, was a great help as well.

Finally, thanks to my wife, Peggy, for her support and understanding. It made all the difference. Thank you also to our sports-playing children, Ben and Eli. Ben is mentioned throughout these pages. Eli is a slick baseball player in his own right. Both offered valuable perspectives on how children are affected by a dad who becomes wrapped up in the athletic lives of his kids, as only eyewitnesses could.